MORE DAILY WISDOM

More **DAILY** WISDOM

365 BUDDHIST INSPIRATIONS

edited by Josh Bartok

WISDOM PUBLICATIONS • BOSTON

Wisdom Publications
199 Elm Street
Somerville MA 02144 USA
www.wisdompubs.org

Library of Congress Cataloging-in-Publication Data
More daily wisdom : 365 Buddhist inspirations / edited by Josh Bartok.
      p. cm.
   Includes bibliographical references and index.
   ISBN 0–86171–296–X (pbk. : alk. paper)
   1. Buddhist devotional calendars. 2. Buddhist meditations. I. Bartok, Josh.
BQ5579.M65 2005
294.3'4432—dc22

                                                  2005025139

ISBN0-86171-296-X
First Edition
09   08   07   06   05
5   4   3   2   1

2LR-2OT.2OM

Special thanks to Kristin Lambert whose assistance was instrumental to the preparation of this work.

Cover design by Laura Shaw.
Interior design by Gopa &Ted2, Inc. Set in Weiss 11/15pt.

Wisdom Publications' books are printed on acid-free paper and meet the guidelines for permanence and durability set by the Council of Library Resources.

Printed in Canada.

Dedicated to all members of our human family throughout space and time.

TABLE OF CONTENTS

Preface   ix

Daily Wisdom   1

Bibliography & Index by Book Cited   369

Index by Topic   375

About Wisdom   387

PREFACE

As the Buddha's teachings take deep root and begin to come to fruition in America, we have an unprecedented opportunity. For the first time in history, the many streams of Buddhism flow side by side, in some cases intermingling, and in all cases enriching each other.

We good-hearted seekers responding to the truth of suffering in ourselves and the world are in a position to benefit from centuries—in some cases millennia—of the refined traditions of Buddhist wisdom from all over the world. We are boundlessly lucky to have so many teachers beckoning us further on the path to freedom and great joy. We can hear the ancient Chinese masters of Chan and their modern descendents in the Japanese-derived lineages of Zen; we can be touched by the teachers and treasured ones—lamas and rinpoches—of the Tibetan Vajrayana tradition; we can learn from the renunciants of the School of the Elders, the Theravada tradition; and we can walk together with modern-day monastics and with laypeople striving to manifest the Buddha's teachings in their lives. What's more, we have the opportunity to taste the uniquely Western flavors of teaching, as traditional Buddhism stretches its own boundaries in the dialogue with psychology and psychotherapy, social activism and yoga, Judaism and Christianity.

It is my hope that the diverse teachings in *More Daily Wisdom* will serve as a series of inspirations, invitations to take this dialogue deeply into our own hearts and minds. And it is my intent that the page-a-day format allows you the spaciousness to mine the true treasure of all of these wise words. I hope you find value in this collection. And may we realize the Way together.

Josh Bartok
Somerville, Mass.

A WORD ON WORDS

Certain Buddhist words have entered the English language in their Sanskrit forms, and so for ease of reading, *More Daily Wisdom* uses *Dharma, karma,* and *nirvana* even in places where the author of the book from which an excerpt was taken used the Pali words *Dhamma, kamma,* and *nibbana*.

If we are in a good mood when we get up in the morning, if there is a warm-hearted feeling within, automatically our inner door is opened for that day. Even should an unfriendly person happen along, we would not experience much disturbance and might even manage to say something nice to that person. We could chat with the not-so-friendly person and perhaps even have a meaningful conversation. Once we create a friendly and positive atmosphere, it automatically helps to reduce fear and insecurity. In this way we can easily make more friends and create more smiles.

We may need permission, from time to time, to allow ourselves to relax, to not be so hard on ourselves—to simply be at ease and happy. We need to learn to be kind to ourselves.

If we are true to the steps we take, the travel makes sense and the journey confirms itself.

In mindful gratitude
for such freedom as I have,
may I overcome
ignorance and apathy
and become a force for good.

One appears before one's parents as a child, before one's child as a parent, before one's husband as a wife, before one's wife as a husband. At work, the face and form one takes on depend upon the position one occupies. This is our true form. There is no clump called "I" moving from this spot to that spot, instant by instant. Rather, through particular encounters with particular people, within each encounter, within each transition, something called "I" makes its appearance. Thus it is that what seems to be outside yourself is, in reality, your complement, that which gives this instant of your life its glow.

Hell does not exist from its own side; the negative mind makes it up.

Once I'd achieved my goal I had to admit to myself it wasn't what I expected and that it did not in fact make everything perfect. And this will happen to anyone who attains any kind of "success" no matter how it is defined—even if success is defined as complete, unsurpassed, perfect enlightenment. You will discover upon reaching it that whatever it is, it's not what you expected and nothing is any more perfect than it ever was.

We can be surprised by the "obvious" questions beginners ask that perhaps we ourselves could have asked.

The scriptures say that when the mind indulges in sensual objects, it becomes agitated. This is the usual state of affairs in the world, as we can observe. In their quest for happiness, people mistake excitement of the mind for real happiness. They never have the chance to experience the greater joy that comes with peace and tranquility.

Wherever a person goes, his deeds, like a shadow, will follow.

If a thought arises, take note of it and then dismiss it. When you forget all attachments steadfastly, you will naturally become zazen itself. This is the art of zazen. Zazen is the Dharma-gate of great repose and joy.

The source of our own happiness is within ourselves.

The Buddha stated clearly that saying only what is true is not sufficient for skillful speech. Speaking skillfully also requires saying what is useful for the listener to hear.

No matter how wise and compassionate our teachers may be, they cannot walk the path for us.

D. LOY AND L. GOODHEW IN *THE DHARMA OF DRAGONS AND DAEMONS*

If you want enlightenment, abandon to its depths all ordinary attachment to deeds and behavior, principles and obligations, opinions and interpretations; be as before the birth of your mother and father, separate from all external phenomena, neither sinking into internal quiet nor settling in the void.

When others out of jealousy treat me wrongly with abuse and slander, I shall train to take upon myself the defeat and offer to others the victory.

We say that mental activity is like the deadly poisonous cobra. If we don't interfere with a cobra, it simply goes its own way. Even though it may be extremely poisonous, we are not affected by it; we don't go near it or take hold of it, and it doesn't bite us. The cobra does what is natural for a cobra to do. That's the way it is. If you are clever you'll leave it alone. And so you let be that which is good. You also let be that which is not good—let it be according to its own nature. Let be your liking and your disliking. Treat them the same way as you treat the cobra. Don't interfere.

Love is not something you have or don't have. It is not a possession. It is what you are.

In short, whatever I may do throughout my activities,
I ask, "What is my mind doing?"
Thus, it is the practice of bodhisattvas to accomplish
    the benefit of others
with continuous mindfulness and conscientiousness.

We suffer because we assume we can find happiness only in certain things—and fail to see that the things we love are not confined to a particular time and space, but are always all around us.

MATTHEW BORTOLIN in *THE DHARMA OF STAR WARS*

In asana practice, we can begin to see how reactive we are. As we go deeper into a stretch and the sensations become more intense, just because they are different, we may find ourselves tightening up our muscles, holding our breath, and constricting our mind in aversion. Or we may begin to see how quickly we get attached to pleasant sensations, and how we seek to prolong them and struggle to get them back when they are lost. These reactive behaviors are all the cause of *dukkha*, suffering, and in our practice we can learn how to let them go.

Problems tend to contain within themselves both their causes and their solutions.

Where there is confusion is where peace can arise.
When confusion is penetrated with understanding,
what remains is peace.

In reality, all of us are *nothing but* Buddha nature.

In taking refuge in the Buddha, we return home to the principle of awakening and trust the enlightening ones of the world to guide us, also radically trusting our own true, awakened self. We return home to our deepest, kindest, most dynamic and open self, the self that is fully interconnected and integrated with all others, beyond our conditioned prejudices about our estrangement. This taking refuge is a psychological orientation and direction, and also the fundamental formal ritual and practice of Buddhism.

If I were to sum up the past forty years of my life, the time since I became a monk, I would have to say that it has been an ongoing lesson in the extent of my own stupidity.

SOKO MORINAGA in *NOVICE TO MASTER*

This place of mine
never is entered by humans
come for conversation,
only by the mute moon's light shafts
that slip in between the trees.

If I want happiness, I simply need to stop causing myself suffering and cultivate happiness. How? It is a process of developing awareness, cultivating determination, and actually *doing*. But it is a long and difficult process. Sometimes I am so confused and do not understand these basic, simple facts. Instead, I follow delusions when they arise, give power to them, and expect to have happiness as the result. I continue to do non-virtuous actions and don't know why I'm unhappy.

THUBTEN PEMO (LINDA GROSSMAN) IN *SPIRITUAL FRIENDS*

Fear is finding fault with the future.

We always imagine that there's got to be somewhere else better than where we are right now; this is the great Somewhere Else we all carry around in our heads. We believe Somewhere Else is out there for us if only we could find it. But there's no Somewhere Else. Everything is right here.

From amid the dark labyrinths of samsara, a being arises—always in the human realm—who unravels the intricate tangle of conditions that sustain this process of bondage and thereby discovers, by his own unaided wisdom, the lost path to Nirvana, the unconditioned state of perfect bliss, peace, and freedom. This being is a Buddha.

We are sure to die. This is so true it scarcely bears mentioning, it seems. But it is also true that through the momentum of desire and action we find ourselves always assuming, taking for granted, another gracious stretch of days to wander through—year upon forgiving year in which we may leisurely revise our philosophies, start or close agreeable projects, and maybe settle someday into some kind of religious faith. Unmindful of death, we grow negligent and live like the froth on a splashing stream—disoriented, weightless, and without conviction.

BHIKKHU NYANASOBHANO IN *LONGING FOR CERTAINTY*

Unseen upon inspection,
It itself appears everywhere.

Meditators face a very real danger of coming to prefer the view from the top of a hundred-foot pole to their real life on the ground. But such peak moments, no matter how profound, always end—leaving us with the problem of how to live in accord with the perspective they provide. Unless we learn how to step off the pole, our practice will devolve into a mere addiction to the highs of peak experience.

What arises in interdependence
has no substantial nature.
What is without substantial nature
emerges nowhere at all.

ON HEARING A BELL

From the old temple
on Cold Mountain,
a soft breeze carries
the sound of a far bell.

The tolling subsides
in the stirring of moonlit trees;
dies
in the frost-streaked sky.

In this long night
of Zen meditation,
when the clear bell sounded,
it was my mind.

If this greatest cold does not penetrate into our bones,
how will the fragrance of the plum blossoms pervade
the entire universe?

Falling down is inevitable; it's what we humans do. When I acknowledge this, it brings me to an unguarded kindness and sympathy. Falling makes us human and, if such a thing can happen, it makes us wise. The trick of falling is just falling itself and the only thing we need do is get back up so we're ready when the time comes to fall again.

All phenomena are subsumed under the two truths:
the relative truth is true with respect to delusion,
and the absolute truth is true with respect to true nature.
The definition of "truth" is that it is without deception.
If you know that the two truths are inseparable, like the
     moon in water,
then the extinction of deluded appearance is close at hand.

If we are serious in our desire for a judicial system that heals, we must find a way to divert our focus from punishing guilt to transforming intention.

DAVID R. LOY in *THE GREAT AWAKENING*

Good fiction makes me say, "That's it. That's right. That's how it is." In Buddhist meditation, I also feel like that— I know I'm seeing clearly, coming close to the way things are. Fiction and meditation are forms of attention, giving life to life. We turn our awareness onto the most ordinary details and they begin to sparkle, bop, and shift to flash out unexpected depths.

KATE WHEELER
IN *NIXON UNDER THE BODHI TREE AND OTHER WORKS OF BUDDHIST FICTION*

JUST BOW

Putting my right and left hands together as one, I just bow.
Just bow to become one with Buddha and God.
Just bow to become one with everything I encounter.
Just bow to become one with all the myriad things.
Just bow as life becomes life.

Once you shut off *thatness*, eternal *thisness* remains.

If I am in no way able to bear the pains of the hells, why then don't I give up anger, which is the cause of all that pain?

LOVE'S EXISTENCE

Love, once called *love*, already isn't love.
Where is the word that can name it?
Can it be touched by rosy lips smiling faintly in anguish?
Can it be lighted by autumn eyes reflecting dark sorrow
    behind its tears?
Does it exist beyond shadowless clouds, echoless precipices,
    and the sea that the mind cannot reach?
That land has no boundaries. A lifespan has no time.
The presence of love cannot be known through eyes
    or mind.
Love's secret is known only through your embroidery needle,
    your planted flowers, in your sleep, and in the poet's
    imagination.

A good teacher wants nothing more than to see you stand on your own two feet.

Emptiness is not independent of form, but rather is a *characteristic* of form; emptiness is form's mode of being.

To obey the rules and regulations is to tie yourself without a rope. To act freely and without restraint is heresy and deviltry. To be aware of the mind, making it pure and quiet, is the false Zen of silent contemplation. To arbitrarily ignore causal relations is to fall into a deep pit. To abide in absolute awakening with no darkening is to wear chains with a yoke. Thinking of good and evil is being in heaven and hell. To have views about the Buddha and the Dharma is to be imprisoned inside two iron mountains. Becoming aware of consciousness at the instant it arises is toying with the soul. Practicing concentration in quiet sitting is an action of devils. If you go forward, you will go astray from the essence. If you go back, you oppose the principle. If you neither go forward nor back, your are a dead man breathing. Tell me now, what will you do? Make the utmost effort to attain full realization in this life! Do not abide in misery forever!

MUMON in *THE GATELESS GATE*

Even in one hundred eons,
karma will never be lost.
When the time comes and they meet the conditions,
beings surely will experience the results.

If as an individual meditator you have a sense that your realization of emptiness is deepening, yet there is no corresponding increase in your compassion toward others, then this is perhaps an indication that your understanding of emptiness is not really profound or genuine. What is there to be so admired about a realization of emptiness that does not lead to greater compassion?

When you don't contemplate yourself, how much suffering do you cause for yourself? And how much do you cause for others? These are things we should contemplate as much as we can. If we don't, we keep trying to get, get, get. And then we don't try to let go, to put things aside, to make any sacrifices at all. We just keep trying to get, and the more we get, the more we want.

Many selves are peacefully dwelling within one self; the one body within the many bodies engages the way. Do you want to understand this truth? We must eat rice with the mouth of the assembly; our vitality must be the strength of the assembly. I respectfully hope you will take good care.

No-self becomes something like the square root of minus one, a number so unacceptable for five centuries of mathematics that it was impugned as "imaginary" and derogated as obvious nonsense until required by necessity to solve real problems in the real world.

BHANTE GUNARATANA (WITH JEANNE MALMGREN) IN *JOURNEY TO MINDFULNESS*

Anger is one of the most difficult defilements to overcome; I know this from firsthand experience. When I was a young monk in Ceylon, I gave many sermons on anger and how to control it even as my own anger caused me to lose my temper repeatedly. I'm calling it "my" anger, but that isn't quite right. Anger would invade my mind and overwhelm me and I let it do that, despite the fact that inevitably it made me feel miserable. When I was angry, I felt pain in my chest and burning in my stomach. My eyesight blurred, my reasoning was unclear, and ugly, harsh words came out of my mouth. After I calmed down, always feeling ashamed and foolish, I would reflect on the Buddha's words about anger: "One should give up anger, renounce pride, and overcome all fetters. Suffering never befalls him who clings not to mind and body and is detached. One who checks rising anger as a charioteer checks a rolling chariot, him I call a true charioteer."

FEBRUARY 24

Sometimes silence awakens the inner heart.

IRA SUKRUNGRUANG, "THE GOLDEN MIX"
IN *NIXON UNDER THE BODHI TREE AND OTHER WORKS OF BUDDHIST FICTION*

No matter how hard you try to free yourself, until you see the value of freedom and the pain of bondage, you won't be able to let go.

When encountering a beautiful object, one should consider it to be like a rainbow in summertime: It appears attractive yet is not thought to be truly existent. To so give up attachment is the practice of the bodhisattvas.

Therefore, I say, with the destruction, fading away, cessation, giving up, and relinquishing of all conceiving, all rumination, all I-making, mine-making, and the underlying tendency to conceit, the Tathagata is liberated through not clinging.

It is necessary to have a deep sense of commitment that *I myself* will take up the responsibility to free all other beings from suffering. In order to generate such powerful compassion, one first needs to develop a sense of intimacy and empathy with other sentient beings; without true intimacy, genuine bodhichitta—the altruistic mind of enlightenment—cannot arise.

LEAP DAY

Although the entire wave is made of water,
    the wave is not the water;
Although all of the water may turn into waves,
    the water is still itself.

Long ago in China there was a monk called Ken. One day Ken's master ordered him to carry a letter to a far-off land. Ken lamented his circumstance to one of his seniors, Genjoza: "Now here I am roaming around the country on this trip; there's no way I am going to attain enlightenment like this!"

When he heard this, Genjoza, thrusting all his strength into his words, put himself at the junior monk's disposal: "I will take care of anything that I can take care of for you on this trip," he said. "But there are just five things that I cannot do in your place. I can't wear clothes for you. I can't eat for you. I can't shit for you. I can't piss for you. And I can't carry your body around and live your life for you."

It is said that upon hearing these words, the monk Ken suddenly awakened from his deluded dream and attained a great enlightenment.

Love—whether between life-mates, parents and children, or friends—affirms the loved one for who he or she is. Our love relationships are not about changing another person to fit the ideal of "love" our ego constructs, nor are they about rejecting other persons because, over time, they change, like everything else in life. Love is being truly present with the loyalty, caring, and commitment that confirm the interconnectedness of all beings.

JEAN SMITH IN *NOW! THE ART OF BEING TRULY PRESENT*

When you wash, imagine that you are washing your divine
body with blissful energy instead of washing your mundane,
suffering body with water. Then dress your divine body
with blissful, divine robes instead of ordinary clothes.
If you start your morning like that, the rest of your day
will be much easier.

One day of continuous practice by us becomes the seed
of all the Buddhas; one day of continuous practice by us is
the continuous practice of all the Buddhas. On the basis of
this continuous practice, all the Buddhas are manifested.
Not to continuously practice what is to be continuously
practiced is to hate the Buddha, not venerate the Buddha;
not to continuously practice what is to be continuously
practiced is to hate continuous practice, not be born with the
Buddha and die with the Buddha. Not to continuously
practice what is to be continuously practiced is to not learn
with the Buddha and not practice with the Buddha. Opening
up enlightenment in this present time and letting go of
enlightenment is the action of continuous practice.
Becoming a Buddha and transcending Buddhahood is
the action of continuous practice.

Fundamentally, the basis on which you can build a sense of caring for others is the capacity to love yourself.

I saw in the instant and with great excitement how Gerard Manley Hopkins had formed from a common noun a previously unknown verb, giving to the world a new word: "selves." You can conjugate it: *I selve, you selve, she selves, we are selving.* That's it! I'm a verb not a noun. As useful as the convention might be, reality itself is too alive to be contained by names of person, place, or thing. The whole of this great earth and everything in it is inflected in this way, a movement that "goes itself." "What I do is me." In that line of Hopkins', I was touching the great mystery of a "self" in which the doing is all there is.

Doubt—in everything—is absolutely essential. Every thing, no matter how great, how fundamental, how beautiful or important it is, must be questioned.

When we reflect on old age, illness, death, separation from what we love, and the inheritance we set up for ourselves by our deeds, we nourish the mind with knowledge of the real character of the universe; we are made more serious and more attentive to the potential of our daily actions; we are more prepared to restrain ourselves from error, to recognize what is wholesome, and to do such actions as help ourselves and others.

BHIKKHU NYANASOBHANO IN *LONGING FOR CERTAINTY*

MARCH 9

What matters more than anything is the spirit of the work.

Mundane being and nirvana—
neither one exists.
It is just the thorough knowledge of mundane being
that is spoken of as "nirvana."

In the West, when you are sick you get therapy to cure your illness. Meditation retreats are similar: you put yourself into a certain situation depending upon what the particular problem is. That's why I say that retreat is like medicine: an antidote to both the disease and its symptoms.

It is bad to try to know everything; one should know just the right amount.

The concept of emptiness is like a medicine—a medicine for the illness of naïve realism. But like any medicine, too much of it can make you sick.

Willingly taking on suffering, we will never be overwhelmed by the suffering that we are bound to experience.

MARCH 15

Wearing the monk's robe is not just a tradition or something we do so that people can recognize us as monks. It's more to remind ourselves who we are, what we are supposed to do, and how we should interact with others. It helps us to choose our speech wisely, to avoid overindulgence, and to remember to strive for peace with those around us.

Though forms can be seen, one is not deluded by them. This is clairvoyance. When sounds are heard through the ears, the echo of vibrations is clearly discerned, and yet there is no dependence on discriminating thoughts. This is called clairaudience. When you clearly understand the nature of your mind, you will realize the oneness of the minds of the buddhas, the ancestors, ordinary people, and heavenly beings. This is the power of mind-reading. From the moment you realize your inherent nature, your mind will penetrate the eons of emptiness that preceded creation through to the endless future. Clear and independent, it will not attach itself to the changing phenomena of life and death, past and future, but will remain constant without any obstructing doubts. This is the power of knowing past lives. When you understand the nature of your own mind, it will thoroughly light up the dark cave of ignorance and the original natural beauty will manifest. In an instant you will pass through the ten directions without stopping in the blue sky. This is your inherent nature's true power to fly through the air. When you understand the nature of your own mind, delusions will change into wisdom.

Listen to "the sound of one hand clapping" the next time
you see a couple united in wisdom and love walking hand
in hand.

Real prayer surrenders to the moment. Real prayer opens to life. Real prayer listens deeply. Learn to pray without ceasing.

EZRA BAYDA WITH JOSH BARTOK
IN *SAYING YES TO LIFE (EVEN THE HARD PARTS)*

We can't induce every other person in the world to immediately become more compassionate, so your primary responsibility is to make your own loving-kindness and compassion more open, more impartial.

The world is not something outside of us, something that we view as mere bystanders, lamenting its sorrow and evils. No, what happens to the whole world as such is what happens to our very own True Selves. The sickness of the world is our very own sickness. This is the sickness of the bodhisattva; it is a sickness that is also the hope and salvation of all living beings. In Christian terms it is the reality of the cross of Christ, the bearer of the sufferings of the world. Only one who has experienced this realm, as one with all the crucified of the world, can truly say with Zen Master Yun-men, "Every day is a good day."

RUBEN L.F. HABITO IN *LIVING ZEN, LOVING GOD*

We in the West cannot blindly ignore the horrendous cruelty of the factory-style food production of animals. Because of their living conditions and the modes of their slaughter, animals live in fear, pain, and suffering. To eat the flesh of their bodies is to be fully implicated in their pain—and in the causes and conditions of their terrible state.

I will be free when I tame my own self.

Instead of looking at others and thinking, "She is this, he is that," visualize every person you see as Avalokiteshvara, the bodhisattva of compassion. When you visualize other people as Avalokiteshvara, there's no way you can feel negative toward them. It's impossible. Instead of misery, they give you blissful energy.

Monks, even if bandits were to sever you savagely limb by limb with a two-handled saw, he who gave rise to a mind of hate toward them would not be carrying out my teaching.

MARCH 25

Regardless of where you go or what you do, in one way or another your life is restricted. Don't look to circumstances or environment for your freedom. You won't find it there. Yet you can always find freedom within limitation.

The heart of the bodhisattva is always turned toward other beings. Such a one chooses to place herself in the most difficult situations, and has the energy and natural commitment to harrow souls from the hells that they have created. And she does this with no attachment to outcome, and a spirit of radical optimism.

Compassion is an aspiration, a state of mind, wanting others to be free from suffering. It's not passive—it's not empathy alone—but rather an empathic altruism that actively strives to free others from suffering.

Everything I experience, which appears to my mind to be so solid and static, is, in fact, constantly decaying. It is no more substantial or enduring than the sound of a bell.

THUBTEN DONDRUB (NEIL HUSTON) in *SPIRITUAL FRIENDS*

In the absence of a self-centered or isolated perspective, our moment-to-moment functioning spontaneously manifests our natural embeddedness in life. This "true" self is neither inside nor outside; it is neither an inner life plan nor a union with a greater or transcendent Being. There is nothing "beyond" being just this moment.

History does not unfold in a straight line from creation to apocalypse. It develops, rather, in repetitive cycles of growth and decline nested within the wider cycles of the cosmic process.

BHIKKHU BODHI IN *GREAT DISCIPLES OF THE BUDDHA*

Fear is the major ingredient of pain. It is what makes pain *hurt*. Take away the fear and only feeling itself is left.

Thinkin' about walking down to the corner store, saying hi to the Chinese lady, saying hi to the Buddha. Thinkin' about changing religions out of First Baptist and over into Buddhist. Thinkin' about being a Booo—dist, a Boo—ooooo—dist! Get me a little guy in a gold box. Hang it round my neck and look at it in the mirror. Wave to it. "Hey, Booo-dah! Hey!"

APRIL 2

The Kagyu master Gampopa said:

Although there are such terms as discriminating awareness and mind, they belong to the realm of logic, while the real discriminating awareness or mind is beyond all that can be known and expressed.

Be clear about this: It is very dangerous to be content with the intellectual explanation of Dharma and not to practice. That cannot help you. Many Western and Eastern professors and scholars who admit they don't practice can speak at length on all aspects of Buddhist philosophy. Ask them a question and they can answer. But their explanations are very superficial. When an experienced practitioner talks, his words have a blessed energy. He may be talking about the same thing that the scholars are, but the way he expresses himself touches your heart. The talk of those without experience is like the empty wind whistling about your ears.

LAMA YESHE IN *BECOMING VAJRASATTVA*

A mind deprived of the fresh air of mindfulness grows stale, breathes shallowly, and chokes upon defilements.

Standing up, sitting down, laughing, weeping—these are jewels we don't recognize as our own treasure.

Although this Dharma inheres in each of us in abundance, it does not become visible without practice, nor is it realized without enlightenment. If you let it go, it fills your hand; yet it transcends one and many. If you talk about it, it fills your mouth; yet it is infinite in space and time.

BELLIGERENT SQUASHES

SQUASH ZAZEN

SQUASHES LIVING OUT THE REALITY OF LIFE

DRAWINGS BY KOSHO UCHIYAMA IN OPENING THE HAND OF THOUGHT

Mindfulness notices that some thought has boiled up and is about to take us for a ride—and just doesn't go along with it.

Can we bear to listen to others and hear what we have not confessed to ourselves? Can we hear what we do not know? Can we stir the ocean with the broken stick of our aspirations? Can we free all creations?

No single answer can hold the truth of a good heart.

JOAN HALIFAX in *THE WISDOM OF LISTENING*

Within the structure of every conformity, every confinement and restraint, dwells the heart of the runaway. It is a being spare, swift, original. It speaks words of its own telling, sings songs of its own heart's consent, runs unhindered in fields of its own choosing. It is an unimpaired body and an irrepressible freedom. And it refuses to be forgotten.

When we begin to live a life of Trust in Mind, we cease fearing the fundamental truths of life—impermanence, suffering, and the emptiness of self—and are able to release our minds and bodies into their flow. Then we discover that, precisely because they are always true, these things are a source of refuge. The things that we need to accomplish our awakening are brought to us, and over time, faith grows to complete trust. All is well, all manner of things are well.

APRIL 12

To always view authority with suspicion, to believe it's unhealthy to ever submit to another, to see yourself as wholly independent, to believe you are completely free— this is delusion. And this delusion prevents true learning on the spiritual path. But neither can we place spiritual teachers on pedestals, imagining them saintly, finished, above the travails of our daily world. This delusion that the teacher is perfect arises out of the childish mind that still wants to be saved. But spiritual teachers aren't perfect; they too are ongoing processes. In fact, unless teachers continue to work at their own edge, with their own fears and difficulties, they can no longer be effective teachers, because they are no longer connected with the experience of others.

EZRA BAYDA WITH JOSH BARTOK
IN *SAYING YES TO LIFE (EVEN THE HARD PARTS)*

The only way to real balance within one's self and peace in the world is to face the dark side with openness and courage—and come to terms with the truth of reality as it is.

The difference between "problems" and mere difficulties rests in relating to your situation openly and skillfully. Letting yourself simply experience your difficulties—without getting caught up in thoughts about how much you dislike them and in wishes that you didn't have to deal with them in the first place—will change your experience of difficulties. But be very clear about this: It's not a matter of denying discomfort or resisting unfavorable circumstances; it is simply being willing to relate to all things just as they are—and practicing anyway. Even if your sitting doesn't always come easily—as it surely won't!—just view everything as a helpful lesson, take all experience as it comes, without comment, neither clinging to it nor running away. This is the nature of the practice of sitting.

I do not perceive even one other thing that leads to such great harm as an undeveloped mind. An undeveloped mind leads to great harm.

It was said of the bodhisattvas, the liberative saints of Buddhism, that they could wander around hell as if it were a fairground.

When we become sick, we often take the illness personally and feel that our happiness is conditional upon getting rid of it. We forget the fact that illness—along with aging and death—is a hallmark of our human existence, and we get angry at our bodies for "letting us down." Sometimes, out of fear, we generate horrendous stories about our illness that may cause us more suffering than the illness itself. When we realize that illness is inescapable, realize that stress around illness increases our suffering, and that being sick is not a shortcoming—only then can we be at ease with, and even empowered by, illness.

Without any religious dogma whatsoever, by using simple common sense, it is important to judge what is right and what is wrong, what is happiness and what is unhappiness. We can only really do this if we can understand that the feelings, rights, and needs of others are every bit as important as our own.

Too often what we think right to say is only what the desire or aversion of the moment urges us to say.

If speaking is through speech, if breathing is through breath, if seeing is through the eyes, if hearing is through the ears, if touching is through the skin, if meditation is through the mind, if exhaling is through the outbreath... then who am I?

There has never been anything to reject, nor to accept, nor to transform; everything is contained within mind.

The basic paradox: everything is a mess yet all is well.

If you're looking for mouse turds, that's what you'll find. If you're looking for gold, you'll find that. But if you are looking for your true self, it is not a thing to be found. Exhaust your thoughts and discard whatever you're holding onto, and your true self will naturally be revealed.

GERRY SHISHIN WICK IN *THE BOOK OF EQUANIMITY*

APRIL 24

The means are the ends and the ends are the means.
Nothing matters; everything matters.

The border between worldly activity and pure Dharma practice rests on the question of why you are doing it.

Nirvana is not another place but a liberated way of experiencing this one.

Silence, which is both space and pause, is inherent in all beings. Our body manifests it as pulse, the pause between heartbeats, the point of rest between exhalation and inhalation. Such silence resides in the very tissues of which we are formed: in the spaces separating the material components of our cells, in the structured vacancy that allows for the dance of molecules, in the infinitesimal vastness of the atom where electrons orbit that charged nucleus, in the furthest descent into the micro-being of our existence where matter dissolves into space, and silence is all that is left.

It is always easier to be right than helpful.

It is said that if you understand mind, knowing this one thing
   illuminates everything,
but if you don't understand mind, knowing everything
   obscures the one thing.

To sit with the idea that you are going to gain enlightenment is just ridiculous.

Since our thirst cannot be sated, it must be transformed.

Paying attention to one's breathing in Zen is not simply a physical exercise that keeps one concentrated on a single point, but the very abandonment of one's total being to the Breath of God, here and now. It is letting one's whole self be possessed by the Breath of God, to be vivified, guided, inspired, and fulfilled in it.

Now do a brief meditation: Imagine you are experiencing an intense emotion, such as anger or attachment, toward someone. Then imagine how, caught up in the emotion, you would respond in a scenario involving that person. Analyze how you relate to the object of your anger or attachment, and compare this with how you relate to people in your normal state of mind. Look at the differences between these two scenarios and compare them. This way, you will learn to recognize the psychological process involved in a forceful affliction, such as anger, and appreciate how grasping at reified qualities of the person lies at the root of an afflictive emotion.

Expounding one yard cannot be done without practicing one yard; expounding one foot cannot be done without practicing one foot.

The master in Buddhism is like a rainbow—beautiful to look upon from afar but vanishing when one sees it near at hand.

MAY 6

The Dharma was and is my shield, my umbrella in the worst storms. It's a shelter we can always rely on—if we simply remember to.

The more I doubted, the more I meditated, the more I practiced. Whenever doubt arose, I practiced right at that point. Wisdom arose. Things began to change. It's hard to describe the change that took place. The mind changed until there was no more doubt. I don't know how it changed. If I were to try telling someone, they probably wouldn't understand.

Loving everyone in the whole world is embodied in our love for those closest to us and in compassionate action to care for those in need. This is done one grain of rice at a time—one smile, one touch, or one step at a time. The realization and clear vision of the whole universe contained within each small act expands the heart and enables love to bloom right here and now.

If we fall asleep with a virtuous or noble frame of mind, then the odds are higher that the first thought that springs to mind when we wake up will also be virtuous or noble. That is one aspect of karma—the karmic result of consciously planting a thought in our mind. As a result of that first conscious thought, a new thought may occur that is a reflection of that first thought. It's not the same thought, but something that feels quite similar due to the power of what preceded it. That is how habits are formed. If you fall asleep feeling deeply unhappy, then the moment you wake up there will be some remnant of that feeling. It's not likely that if you go to sleep feeling sad that you will wake up feeling full of joy. Isn't that true?

If you miss *this*, you miss it all.

Remember what I have left undeclared as undeclared, and
    remember what I have declared as declared. And what have
    I left undeclared?

"The world is eternal"—I have left undeclared.

"The world is not eternal"—I have left undeclared.

"The world is finite"—I have left undeclared.

"The world is infinite"—I have left undeclared.

"The soul is the same as the body"—I have left undeclared.

"The soul is one thing and the body another"—I have left
    undeclared.

"After death a Tathagata exists"—I have left undeclared.

"After death a Tathagata does not exist"—I have left
    undeclared.

"After death a Tathagata both exists and does not exist"—
    I have left undeclared.

"After death a Tathagata neither exists nor does not exist"—
    I have left undeclared.

Why have I left that undeclared? Because it is unbeneficial,
it does not belong to the fundamentals of the spiritual life,
it does not lead to disenchantment, to dispassion, to cessation,
to peace, to direct knowledge, to enlightenment, to Nirvana.
That is why I have left it undeclared.

All that we are attached to is impermanent—so there's nothing to get ruffled about.

Every unfortunate situation that we encounter is a result of our own karma and delusions that propel us endlessly through cyclic existence. There is no one to blame but ourselves.

Not liking it here you go traveling over there; not liking it there you come touring back here. That's all there is to it, following your noses everywhere. You don't have to do a lot of traveling around; just stay here and develop the practice, learn it in detail. Make an effort, all of you.

The object of practice is not transcendence but transformation, yet ultimately we must transcend ourselves.

FRANCIS DOJUN COOK (ELUCIDATING DOGEN) IN *HOW TO RAISE AN OX*

It is through embracing our suffering that we discover transcendence from it. It is by accepting life as it is in its gains and losses, its joyful times and its sorrowful times, that we reside in a place of peace and freedom. This is the ultimate truth of nirvana.

The difference between samsara and nirvana is a state of mind.

When you visit someone in hospital, talk to the person
and leave the doctors and nurses to talk to the sickness.

There is no miserable place waiting for you, no hell realm, sitting and waiting like Alaska—waiting to turn you into ice cream. But whatever you call it—hell or the suffering realms—it is something that you enter by creating a world of neurotic fantasy and believing it to be real. It sounds simple, but that's exactly what happens.

When you have a problem, think about it. Then think about it some more. And then think about it still more and after you've thought all you can think about it, then think non-thinking. When you touch the *origin* of thinking, this is non-thinking. Our practice is neither about thinking nor non-thinking. Let go of your cherished opinions and cultivate the mind of "not-knowing" and the True Dharma will appear.

Inner awareness unblocks outer responsiveness, freeing us to respond wholeheartedly, without fearing failure or loss of self-control. Instead of identifying with our response we can allow the response to reflect the situation. As occasion requires, we can be temperate extremists or passionate moderates, radical conservatives or reasonable revolutionaries.

We can know intellectually the properties of electricity,
but that's nothing like being hit with a live wire.
Realization in Zen is like this.

You should always consider whether there is a way to avoid doing harm.

Training the mind is refined work. Even when knowledge arises, if you decide on your own that it's right for sure, you've failed the test.

If, while devoting yourself to practice, you have thoughts of gain, and thinking it will prevent the interference from demons, you recite invocations from sutras—this kind of reasoning will immediately create a demon inside you, attracting demons from the outside, and causing chaos within.

As for the inevitability of death, we have to remember that it's not just the body that grows old, decays, and dies. Our feelings and mental states do the same thing. If you close your eyes for just one minute, you can experience how a feeling or emotion is born, grows old, and passes away. It's like a wave, rising to a peak and then breaking apart. In the same way, our perceptions grow old and die. Our thoughts grow old and die. Our consciousness grows old and dies. This is the nature of our existence, and it's happening every moment.

Your "true nature" includes everything, even the parts of
yourself you don't like.

A beginner foolishly aims to empty his mind and tries to drive all thoughts away. But *aiming* and *trying* are also thoughts! So aiming and trying keep one from one's goal of becoming emptiness itself. When you think you are in emptiness, you are not in emptiness. When you think you have discovered your Buddha nature, you are far away from it. When no thought arises, there is no need to drive thoughts away. When nothing is born, nothing dies. When nothing is good, nothing is bad. What you never had, you will never miss. What you do not see does not disappear. What cannot increase cannot decrease. This is true emptiness. This is samadhi. When you enter into this condition, you are walking in the Palace of Realization. Never to think—even for a moment—that you are enlightened: *This* is the ideal of Zen meditation.

If we study but don't practice, we won't get results. It's like a man who raises chickens but doesn't collect the eggs. All he gets is the chicken shit! To get the best results you must study and practice as well.

If we sow the seeds of malice toward others, we will find ourselves reaping plenty of it ourselves.

Everything has to do with attitude.

Because of the fundamental equality of all beings in having this natural aspiration to be happy and to overcome suffering, we can develop empathy and strong compassion toward each and every being. By training our mind by focusing on specific beings—friends, enemies, and neutral people—we will be able to extend compassion toward everyone. This point is critical. Otherwise, we risk having the idea that there are faceless sentient beings out there toward whom we can develop compassion, and then we fail to generate any compassion toward the *real* people with whom we have direct contact.

Change the world, change your mind, change yourself.
It is all connected.

Thoughts are all the same. They are just like water bubbles. You see them, but then there is nothing there.

Years ago at the San Diego Zen Center everyone was invited to say a few words about the difference practice had made in their lives. The first few speakers spoke earnestly of the psychological changes they had experienced over the years, their increased patience, compassion, self-awareness—but one woman brought the house down by saying simply, "My apartment is much cleaner."

BARRY MAGID in *ORDINARY MIND*

If we lose our opportunity to dedicate our merit, we run
the risk of destroying great amounts of virtue with our
powerful negative emotions. Our negative emotions are
like monkeys, and our virtue is like oranges and bananas
inside the house. If we are not very careful to close the
door, our negative emotions jump inside and grab
everything for themselves. Our dedication of merit is
like closing the door.

The now of activity is not the self's primordial being, eternal and immutable, nor is it something that enters and leaves the self. The Way, called now, does not precede activity; as activity is realized, it is called now.

When people take the trouble to breathe fresh air, good health proves to them the value of their effort. So too, a meditator who has experienced deep practice, even nirvana, will truly know what mindfulness is worth.

To spend your life being blinded and dragged around by
your own desires is a pathetic thing. However you live, what
you do with your life depends on you. With that
understanding, just sit silently for ten years, then for another
ten, and after that, for ten more years.

KOSHO UCHIYAMA in *OPENING THE HAND OF THOUGHT*

A society where people do not feel that they benefit from sharing with each other has already begun to break down.

With realization, all things are of one family,
without realization, everything is separate and different.
Without realization, all things are of one family,
with realization, everything is separate and different.

JUNE 11

The Sangha is constituted by those people who understand the Dharma and are practicing it seriously. They are the companions of all those who seek to follow the Buddha's path. By virtue of their own practice they are able to support the practice of others and help those who encounter problems. They are like nurses who are able to help in the healing process because they understand the remedy that the doctor has prescribed. Because they are taking the medicine themselves, they are able to show others exactly how to follow the instructions of the perfect doctor, the Buddha. Because they are on the right path, if we follow them and emulate them we will be led toward emancipation. This is why the Sangha, the community of spiritual friends, is a proper refuge.

The diligence of profound love doesn't wait for any reward or reciprocation.

Directly it is said that not a single thing exists, and yet we see in the entire universe nothing has ever been hidden.

Do not yearn for the past: you must practice without finding fault with the present.

There are three ways to take refuge in the Buddha. In *outer refuge*, the Buddha in whom we take refuge is somebody other than ourselves: a person who has attained buddhahood, an enlightened being such as Shakyamuni Buddha. *Inner refuge* is taking refuge in the buddha you yourself will become. *Secret refuge* is the third way of taking refuge. This way of taking refuge is the most difficult of all. You have to recognize that your nervous system is pervaded by blissful energy instead of the usual ridiculous energy of gravitational attachment to sense pleasures, and you take refuge in that. If you do not know how to take refuge properly, whatever meditation you do will be like snow on the road, which looks very impressive as it falls, but quickly disappears.

You believe your opinions; you believe your judgments; you believe your emotions. And these beliefs become your ego— but this ego is not you.

EZRA BAYDA WITH JOSH BARTOK
IN *SAYING YES TO LIFE (EVEN THE HARD PARTS)*

You don't need to look somewhere else or to someone else. Take a good look for yourself. See yourself, for yourself. You are not Buddha. Don't try to be Buddha. Be the best *you* you can be, with all your frailties, sensitivities, and strengths.

When you dream of an elephant, does an elephant appear to your mind? Indeed it appears very clearly. Is there an elephant there? No. This appearance of an elephant in your dream is a union of appearance and emptiness. It appears, yet it does not exist—yet it appears. It is the same with all external phenomena. If we understand the example of the appearance of something in a dream, it is easier to understand how the mind appears yet does not exist, and does not exist yet appears.

With whom shall I battle, for I am my own enemy?
Who will save whom, for I am my own savior?
I am my own witness, for my actions and inactions.

An old friend shared with me an illuminating and marvelously nonlinear teaching that our past lives in our "next life" may well be different from our past lives in this one.

The way of Zen began without the establishment of any sect. It is simply a religion that points to the one original mind of all buddhas and ordinary people. This mind is nothing other than Buddha-nature. To see this nature is what is meant by religious practice. When you realize your Buddha-nature, wrong relationships will instantly disappear, words will be of no concern, the dust of the Dharma will not stain you. This is what is called Zen.

You have to become fed up with your dislikes *and* your likes, your suffering *and* your happiness. Don't you see that this is the very essence of the Dharma?

We need religion in order to develop both this inner peace and peace among the world's traditions; that is the essential role of religion today. And in pursuit of this goal, harmony among the different traditions becomes essential.

Nonattachment is not about being aloof. It is about, for example, loving and accepting your child's behavior when it does not gratify your sense of how *your* child should behave. It is about your having genuine acceptance, even though you are a college professor, of your son's decision to become an auto mechanic—no *ifs, ands,* or *buts.* Or, to give a more difficult example, it is about sustaining compassionate equanimity while your child goes through the throes of manic-depression. Are you able to do what you can without deluding yourself that there is nothing wrong with your child, because you can't handle knowing the truth? Can you act without suffering the shame of having a child who is so "inappropriate" and "dysfunctional"? Nonattachment even means not feeling pride if your child gets into Harvard. Imagine life without shame or pride.

SARA L. WEBER IN *PSYCHOANALYSIS AND BUDDHISM*

May I mindfully acknowledge
that others, like myself, are still growing spiritually,
and forgive their past offenses,
as I forgive my own,
so that I can know
the blessing of a loving heart.

Every thought, word, and deed plants seeds in our minds that will necessarily ripen as fruit: negative actions ripen as suffering, positive actions ripen as happiness. There is nothing that living beings experience that isn't the result of what they've done before.

ROBINA COURTIN in *BECOMING THE COMPASSION BUDDHA*

The word *samadhi* carries within itself two absolutely contrary meanings: "perfect reception" and "perfect non-reception." In order to "perfectly receive" each instant as it occurs, it is necessary to "perfectly not-receive" the previous instant and the future instant. No matter how accurately and in what detail a mirror may reflect what is before it in one instant, should it be turned to face a new direction, the previous reflection will disappear without a trace and the mirror will faithfully reflect what is newly before it. Likewise, in its power to always perfectly receive what is at hand and to perfectly not-receive what is not at hand, the heart functions doubly. For this reason, from times of old, the heart has been likened to a mirror. The state in which this power functions to receive everything perfectly, just as it is—that is to say, the heart of perfect nonreception that does not get caught up—is called "the heart that is still," or simply *Zen*.

SOKO MORINAGA in *NOVICE TO MASTER* ┆ 179

The moment you think only of yourself, the focus of your whole reality narrows, and because of this narrow focus, uncomfortable things can appear huge and bring you fear and discomfort and a sense of feeling overwhelmed by misery.

Unconditional love accepts the impermanent nature of its loved one. It understands that people change, and it adjusts to those changes without selfish demands or pressures.

Most perceived problems merely become problems because we believe that they are so. This is true even of extremes such as disease, old age, and death, which are after all universal and inevitable. It's equally true of the sorrow and grief that often accompanies these events. To define the universal experiences of our species as problems is to define the whole human life system as a problem. And when something is seen as a problem, you feel compelled to do something about it. A problem, like a leaking faucet or a flat tire, is something that needs to be fixed. You can exhaust your life in the effort to fix it.

Dharma transmission is what happens when your sight clears enough that you can see what your teacher and the Buddha have already seen: things as they are.

To release attachments to our actions means they become *choices* we are free to make rather than addictions we blindly follow.

If you have a bad opinion of yourself, it's not a true picture, and you will only make your life difficult. As soon as you start accepting yourself as you are, you begin to transform. In a reasonable way, bring your good qualities to mind and try to develop a positive attitude toward life. With this as your foundation you will be more successful, more positive, and more realistic. This will lead to spiritual growth. It's a very practical way to be.

One famous Buddhist depiction of reality is the Net of Indra, the Indian creator deity. In this metaphor the universe is described as a vast net, and at each junction where the meshes meet sits a jewel. Each jewel reflects the light of all the jewels around it; and all of those jewels reflect others around them. In this way, the whole universe of jewels is ultimately reflected in every single jewel. This holographic image expresses our deep intimacy and interrelatedness with everything in the universe. Given this truth, the goal of universal liberation is simply a realistic approach.

TAIGEN DAN LEIGHTON IN *FACES OF COMPASSION*

There is only this. Mind is transmitted by Mind,
but no one understand this at all.

For playing joyfully in samadhi, the upright sitting position in meditation is the right gate.

JULY 7

Everything that seems to be happening to "you" and "me" is already like a fiction, from a Buddhist's standpoint, and the thing to do is to unravel your involvement in the story, not become entranced and follow it to the end.

Fundamentally, no matter what kind of circumstances we may have fallen into, we are always in the midst of enlightenment. To the extent that we live in the world of letting go of all our own puny ideas, we live in the middle of enlightenment. As soon as we open the hand of thought and let go of our own insignificant ideas, we begin to see that this is so.

The Buddha compared the training of the mind to holding a bird in your hand. The mind is like a tiny bird, and the question is how to hold the bird so that it doesn't fly away. If you hold it too tightly, it will die in your grip. If you hold it too loosely, the tiny bird will slip out through your fingers. So how are you going to hold it so that it doesn't die and doesn't get away?

Acts of compassion have no "meaning" in the sense of validating anything in the bodhisattva; acts of compassion are just acts of compassion and do not need a reason or justification. They become *truly* acts of compassion when the bodhisattva is simultaneously aware that these acts of compassion in samsara are just as empty as anything else, including the bodhisattva herself. Buddhist traditions, including Zen, work creatively and gloriously with this paradox.

When doing zazen don't be upset as thoughts occur, but don't savor them either. Just trace them back to their origin, looking at the source without letting it disturb you.

We are free ourselves insofar as our lives become more playful. Playing is what we are doing when we do not need to gain something from a situation.

D. LOY AND L. GOODHEW IN *THE DHARMA OF DRAGONS AND DAEMONS*

The wanderer Vacchagotta asked the Blessed One:

"When a monk's mind is liberated thus, Master Gotama,
    where is he reborn after death?"
"'Is reborn' does not apply, Vaccha."
"Then he is not reborn, Master Gotama?"
"'Is not reborn' does not apply, Vaccha."
"Then he both is reborn and is not reborn, Master Gotama?"
"'Both is reborn and is not reborn' does not apply, Vaccha."
"Then he neither is reborn nor is not reborn, Master Gotama?"
"'Neither is reborn nor is not reborn' does not apply,
    Vaccha."

All-embracingness, acceptance of all in equality, recognition of each in its uniqueness, and universal availability and responsibility according to every need—these are the four characteristics of the wisdom of the mirrorlike enlightened mind.

RUBEN L.F. HABITO IN *LIVING ZEN, LOVING GOD*

Whenever you feel annoyed, whenever your mind goes bad, just say, "So!" When you feel better, just say, "So!" If you love someone just say, "So!" When you feel you're getting angry, just say, "So!" Do you understand? You don't have to go looking into the scriptures. Just "So!" Whatever arises, just tell it, "So!" It saves a lot of time.

Sincerity and faith are not things that come from outside or inside; they are only acquired by valuing the Dharma and transforming oneself completely.

Our yoga-Dharma practice can be our vocation. The word *vocation* originally meant "to put your voice forth" into the world. What a wonderful way to see our practice. To commit to this practice is to put forth our voice into the world, to truly declare our values and our volition regarding how we relate to life itself. This is what is meant by our practice being our life.

Our attitudes reflect thoughts and emotions, and our thoughts and emotions reflect two principal drives: attraction and repulsion. If we perceive a thing, person, or event to be undesirable, we will react with repulsion and try to avoid it. This repulsion becomes the basis for hostility and other associated negative emotions. If, on the other hand, we find a thing, person, or event desirable, we will react with attraction and try to hold on to it. This attraction becomes the basis for craving and attachment. These basic dynamics of attraction and repulsion form the basis of our engagement with the world. If we think along these lines, it will become clear that when we make statements such as "Today I feel happy" or "Today I feel unhappy," it is only emotions of attachment or aversion that determine which of these is the case.

Although we may have trouble saying just what a nonselfcentered response to life looks like in any given situation, we can be clear what it is *not*. Nonselfcenteredness is not what we ordinarily mean by self-effacement, and it certainly isn't masochistic self-sacrifice. The Buddha's ideal of compassion does not mean dedicating one's life to saving all beings *minus one*.

What does it mean to renounce the world? Renouncing means becoming more reasonable through knowing the characteristic nature of pleasure and of the objects of pleasure.

When angry thoughts arise vividly,
if you look at them nakedly and rest without fabrication,
they will vanish in their own ground without harm
    or benefit.
Self-arising wisdom is none other than that.

It's your life. Just let it be so. As Maezumi Roshi used to say: "You're doing it anyway. You might as well as appreciate it."

Using the tooth-cleaner every morning,
may I vow with all sentient beings,
to attain teeth strong enough
to gnaw away all passions.

The wisdom that develops naturally from nonattachment is knowing how to be content with what we have.

Without understanding the nature of these two truths—
the conventional and the ultimate—it is difficult to fully
appreciate the distinction between appearance and reality,
that is, the discrepancy we experience between our
perception and the way things really are. Without a deep
understanding of this fact, we won't be in a position to get
at the root of our fundamental ignorance.

I have here a commentary on the Diamond Sutra which is, I think, the best of all commentaries. It is hidden within these Buddhist beads. Those who wish to read it, step inside any bead and study it to your heart's content!

LOVE'S REASONS

It's not for nothing that I love you.
Others love my rosy complexion, but you love my gray hair.

It's not for nothing that I long for you.
Others love my smile, but you love my tears.

It's not for nothing that I wait for you.
Others love my vigor, but you love my death.

To take the unsettled self in hand, under whatever conditions, and return to the mind with which one set out; to pick oneself up again, after the mind changes, weakens, and breaks down, and stiffen the determination; to carry through the oft-reconstructed original vow—isn't this the true meaning of courage?

Attachment is a honey-covered razor blade: we are
convinced it's the prelude to pleasure, but in fact,
it leads to nothing but pain.

Compassion is the gift of oneself, the willingness to show up, to bear witness, to be with others. It's not about mistakes or about being right or wrong. It's better than that.

Zazen isn't about blissing out or going into an alpha brain-wave trance. It's about facing who and what you really are, in every single goddamn moment.

And you aren't just bliss, I'll tell you that right now. You're a mess. We all are. But here's the thing: that mess is itself enlightenment.

The most important thing to understand about exertion in practice is that the long term is more important than the short term. It is not as important to make a heroic effort on a given day to practice when you are exhausted as it is to practice steadily over a long time.

Although we may be able to behave to some extent differently than we feel, any successful coercion to feel other than we actually feel—even a coercion to fit some preferred version of ourselves—will keep us at a distance from our true selves.

At the very moment when a good deed is accomplished, all good invariably comes forth. Formless as the myriad kinds of good may be, a good act, wherever it is done, assembles them all, faster than a magnet attracts iron. Its force is stronger than a stormy wind that destroys everything in the universe. Even the great earth, mountains and rivers, even the world, countries and lands, as well as karma-accelerating forces, cannot hinder this confluence of all good.

AUGUST 4

Listening to the dying takes us to the edge of our own fears, for when we open our hearts to someone, we open ourselves to their death. Death will come in with a force equal to the resistance we have to it.

All of us—any of us—can develop infinitely; and any of us can attain buddhahood. The mind we possess right now, though it may be full of ignorance and suffering, can eventually become the mind of an enlightened being, of a buddha.

Everywhere life is sufficient. Just be who you are,
and don't restrict it.

We construct ourselves by what we choose to do. Just as my body is composed of the food I eat, so my character is built by my conscious decisions.

DAVID R. LOY IN *THE GREAT AWAKENING*

Zen practice offers us this paradox: a discipline that promises freedom, a hierarchical relationship that fosters true independence, a form that gives formlessness, a transformation that allows everything to be just as it is.

Remaining trapped in the world of preferences we are led to an expectation of how things *should* be. When our expectation of how things should be conflicts with how things are, there is *dukkha,* suffering.

We wonder how people can't see the most obvious things about themselves—yet we forget those people are us!

Having not yet seen into his own nature, a person sinks in the sea of passion and discrimination, killing his own Buddha mind. This is the murder of murders. That's why keeping the true precepts is the enlightened way of seeing into your own nature. When deluded thoughts arise, you damage the Dharma treasure, destroy its merit, and hence become a thief. When you give rise to deluded thoughts, you cut off the seeds of Buddhahood and continue the life, death, and rebirth–causing karmic activities. This is what is meant by adultery. When you are blinded by deluded thoughts, you forget your precious Dharma body, and seeing only illusion, you call it your body. This is what is meant by lying. Isolated by deluded thoughts you lose sight of your inherent wisdom and become frantic. This is what is meant by being intoxicated. The other precepts should be understood similarly.

There's no need to go searching for anything special;
just live normally. But know where your mind is. Live
mindfully and comprehend clearly. Let wisdom be your
guide; don't live indulging in your moods. Be heedful
and alert. If there is nothing, that's fine; when something
arises, investigate and contemplate it.

You should entreat trees and rocks to preach the Dharma,
and you should ask rice fields and gardens for the truth.
Ask pillars for the Dharma, and learn from hedges and walls.

When you allow your rough edges, your desire to control, your desire to be right, your self-centered view of the world, to fall away, you become who you truly are. You become more fully your own unique self. Both meditation and relationships are powerful opportunities to learn about who you are and to act accordingly.

The various sufferings are just like the death of one's child in a dream; how very tiring to grasp illusory appearances as being real!

In our society there is certainly evil: murders, kidnappings, and other horrible crimes, as well as the many subtler ways people can be cruel to each other. The typical conclusion is that these acts, when they are perpetrated by and happen to other people, have nothing to do with us. We believe they are the deeds of a deranged few and that their effects are limited to certain victimized individuals. But when we perceive the world clearly, we see that *we* are in the murderer and the murderer is us. We are in the victim and the victim is us. We share our community with everyone living in it. If one person in our community is in so much pain that she feels compelled to kill another human being, we need to investigate how our society operates and how, with our participation or our inaction, it has contributed to her unhealthy state of mind.

It isn't so terrible to think logically and to be analytical; if we are designing a bridge or balancing a checkbook, that's the best way to think and the best way to be. But when we look carefully, we see that discursive, linear thinking is only useful for certain kinds of tasks; for others it is quite useless. Like the hammer or the toothbrush, discursive thought is a tool intended for certain kinds of jobs: If you use a hammer to brush your teeth, or a toothbrush to drive nails you are not likely to meet with great success. The problem for most of us born into this culture is that we are strongly conditioned and taught, from infancy onward, to rely almost totally upon discursive logic and rational thought.

JOHN DAISHIN BUKSBAZEN IN ZEN MEDITATION IN PLAIN ENGLISH

Do not give "clarifications" of others' negative acts and shortcomings; this prevents your realization.

There was a king who rounded up all the persons in the city who were blind from birth. He showed the blind men an elephant. To some of the blind men he presented the head of the elephant, to some the ear, to others a tusk, the trunk, the body, a foot, the hindquarters, the tail, or the tuft at the end of the tail. And to each one he said, "This is an elephant." The king then went to the blind men and asked them, "Tell me, blind men, what is an elephant like?" Those who had been shown the head of the elephant replied, "An elephant, your majesty, is just like a water jar." Those who had been shown the ear replied, "An elephant is just like a winnowing basket." Those who had been shown the tusk replied, "An elephant is just like a plowshare." Those who had been shown the trunk replied, "An elephant is just like a plow pole." Those who had been shown the body replied, "An elephant is just like a storeroom." And each of the others likewise described the elephant in terms of the part they had been shown. Even so, monks, are the wanderers of other sects blind and sightless, and thus they become quarrelsome, disputatious, and wrangling, wounding each other with verbal darts.

No matter how powerful a particular teaching may be or how "correct" a philosophical view may be, if it is not suitable to the individual hearing it, it has no value.

You must proceed with great determination, which means
sticking to practice with true courage. In the Japanese
language, *determination* is composed of two ideographs that
carry the respective meanings "to be angry" and "aspiration."
Your anger is not directed toward someone else. Indignant
with yourself over your own weakness and immaturity, you
employ the strong whip of aspiration. This is determination.

What we are now is the result of what we have done, said, and thought before, and what we will be in the future is thus in our own hands. We are the boss.

It is the inmost nature of nature to change, and to change absolutely. Nothing can be held back, nothing kept, nothing saved. And however distressing this might seem to us, our survival lies in such radical regeneration, the workings of which are generous beyond the count of loss or gain.

We come to think there is a method, a rational way to get us from here to there, all the while confirming a view that where we are is somehow wrong or insufficient.

Everything depends upon your mind.

We are all as much the creation of those around us as we are independent beings in our own right.

Your pleasure is limited because you function within the framework of duality. If you dismantle this framework, you will experience limitless joy.

The inner enemy is the trigger that unleashes the destructive power of the external enemy. As long as these inner enemies remain secure within, there is great danger.

The fundamental ground of our lives, our true human nature, may be called generative emptiness charged with potential. The many beings distinctively present it: the bird sings it, our child whines it, the wind blows it, our stomach growls it; the extraordinary is not *apart from* but part and parcel *of* ordinary moments of living and dying.

JOSEPH BOBROW in *PSYCHOANALYSIS AND BUDDHISM*

Though you may speak of Mind or the objective world,
and though you may speak of defilement or awakening,
these are all just names for one's true Self.

AUGUST 31

I make life what it is; life makes me what I am.

Your mind applies itself universally, everywhere. It sees colors with the eyes, hears voices with the ears, smells odors with the nose, forms words with the mouth, grips with the hands, runs with the feet. All buddhas and ordinary people have this blessed power.

The difference between samsara and nirvana is that samsara is the world experienced as a sticky web of attachments that seem to offer something we lack—a grounding for our groundless sense of self.

DAVID R. LOY IN *THE GREAT AWAKENING*

The mind cannot exist within the body, as the body,
or somewhere in between; nor can the mind exist wholly
independent of the body. Such a mind is not to be found;
the mind is therefore devoid of intrinsic existence.
And when beings recognize this nature of their mind,
liberation can take place.

Letting go of conditioning while steeped in completely relaxed awareness, one is able to act effectively, innocent of grasping and attachments.

Quietness is an element in meditation, but merely striving to attain quietness leads nowhere. It is like putting a paper bag over a cat's head: it will walk backward, never advance.

We're all subject to karma, to cause and effect, birth and decay. But how can we be peaceful no matter what conditions our karma brings? That's the challenge of our practice. To liberate ourselves from our karma we must become karma itself.

SEPTEMBER 7

Behind attachments is freedom. Behind fear, love. Behind desire, the quiet joy of being.

EZRA BAYDA WITH JOSH BARTOK
IN *SAYING YES TO LIFE (EVEN THE HARD PARTS)*

251

No matter how "noble" or "justified" our negative emotions may seem, we must acknowledge that indulging them merely plants the karmic seeds for later pain.

The less we know of Dharma, the more the mind will continually pursue mental impressions. Feeling happy, it succumbs to happiness. Feeling suffering, it succumbs to suffering. It's constant confusion!

SEPTEMBER 10

When you are alive, be completely alive, and when you are dying, die thoroughly.

FRANCIS DOJUN COOK (ELUCIDATING DOGEN) IN *HOW TO RAISE AN OX*

SEPTEMBER 11

Destructive acts are motivated by disturbed states of mind, that is to say, by a mind dominated by the afflictions. In the entire history of human society, it is these mental afflictions, these undisciplined states of mind, that underlie all of humanity's destructive acts—from the smallest act of swatting a fly to the greatest atrocities of war. We must remember that ignorance itself is an affliction.

No matter how much we may love our partner, we cannot take away our partner's pain, we cannot "make" our partner happy, and we cannot "enlighten" our partner. Each person must walk the spiritual path for her- or himself. So even if we travel together, we travel alone. Recognizing this aloneness is essential for togetherness.

SEPTEMBER 13

Right effort and deep commitment should not be harsh. They are practices of ease and compassion.

The moment you were born was you. The moment you die
will be you. This moment right now is you. There is no
difference between this moment and yourself. You live
through a million you/moments every single second.
Being and time are not two things.

"I am" is a conceiving; "I am this" is a conceiving;
"I shall be" is a conceiving; "I shall not be" is a conceiving;
"I shall have a physical form" is a conceiving; "I shall be
formless" is a conceiving. Conceiving is a disease,
conceiving is a tumor, conceiving is a dart. By overcoming
all conceivings, one is called a sage at peace.

The foolish and the ignorant are bound to emotional choices
that in turn attach them more fiercely to their ignorance.
The wise person, on the other hand, walks through life
unswayed and nonreactive, yet free to act compassionately
and with equanimity.

We try so hard to preserve the very thing that's making us miserable. We cling hard to our pain because we mistakenly think that that pain is who we really are. We define ourselves by what we don't like or we define ourselves by what we like. Either way we miss the truth. We harbor some inexplicable fear that if we start to enjoy everything about life without picking and choosing we might somehow cease to exist.

Even as you maintain mindfulness and alertness, thoughts of attachment, aversion, and bewilderment will still arise because the habits that produce their arising have not yet been completely eradicated. Nevertheless, if you have some recognition of your mind's nature, then, when any one of those thoughts arises, you will experience the mind's true nature in that thought, because the mind's nature is also the nature of that thought.

When expression is uttered, nonexpression is unuttered. If you recognize that expression is uttered in its fullness, and yet do not experientially penetrate nonexpression as nonexpression, you are still short of attaining the original face and marrowbones of the Buddhas and ancestors.

What I do and what happens to me are not events that occur in time; they are the forms that my being-time takes.

D. LOY AND L. GOODHEW IN *THE DHARMA OF DRAGONS AND DAEMONS*

SEPTEMBER 21

AUTUMN NIGHT,
THINKING OF A TZU-KE MOUNTAIN MONK

With the whole mountain
colored by rain,
its form is hard to see.

From across the river,
the chanting of sutras
is difficult to hear.

On Tzu-ke Peak,
deep in the night,
many monks enter *samadhi*.

But at the stone tower,
who is sweeping
the autumn clouds?

Without turning your back on a thousand people or ten thousand people, drop off body and mind, go to the hall, and sit zazen.

Though your heart may feel small, it is spacious beyond the mind's imagination.

The spaciousness of the heart can hold the suffering of the world.

EZRA BAYDA WITH JOSH BARTOK
IN *SAYING YES TO LIFE (EVEN THE HARD PARTS)*

There is no ice and snow apart from water, and the buddhahood of ordinary people can be likened to snow and ice melting to become water.

At each moment you stand at a crossroads between the worldly way and the Dharma way. Which way will you choose? If you are to be liberated, it is at this point.

The choice is yours to make.

Regardless of how fine a teacher you have or where you got your fine ideas, if you cling to any of them, you're trapped!

Don't draw another's bow;
Don't ride another's horse;
Don't speak of another's faults;
Don't inquire into another's affairs.

SEPTEMBER 28

We do not exist in isolation. Rather, all beings are intimately interrelated in our effects on each other. We are the product of our genetic and cultural inheritance; of the intricate web of influence of family, friends, and acquaintances; and of innumerable other unknowable conditions that bring us to our present state.

Suffering is nothing but existence enslaved to ignorance.

Enlightenment is liberation from the dross of learning and experience that, without one's being aware of it, has accumulated and settled like so much sediment— or like cholesterol into one's arteries! It is the vivid, lively manifestation of the heart with which one is born— the heart that is no-form, no-mind, nonabiding, attached neither to form nor to thought, but in dynamic motion. Consequently, enlightenment is not an endpoint, but rather a place to start.

SOKO MORINAGA in *NOVICE TO MASTER*

To eliminate the destructive potential of anger and hatred entirely, we need to recognize that the root of anger lies in the attitude that cherishes our own welfare and benefit while remaining oblivious to the well-being of others. This self-centered attitude underlies not only anger, but virtually all our states of mind. It is a deluded attitude, misperceiving the way things actually are, and this misperception is responsible for all the suffering and dissatisfaction that we experience.

One characteristic of a life lived from a thoroughly non-dualistic perspective is that *we no longer have any problems.* That is, we no longer divide our life into the good parts and the problematic parts; there is simply *life,* one moment after another. Problems don't disappear *from* our life, they disappear *into* our life.

This fleeting teeny-weeny present moment is the *only* time in which you are free to act. Within the confines in which our past action has placed us, we are absolutely free *right now*.

That's an important point—make sure you see it.

Can you face the wall without facing the wall?

The earth provides not just a little, but all. The very body
and mind with which I tend the earth are themselves of
the earth. I am but earth tending earth. Were the earth
not to roll this garden toward the sun today, were the
clouds not to gather above the sea, the waters not to flow,
the soil not to brim with its billions of microorganisms,
were all or any part of this to fail, I would fail as well,
my body numbed to a fixed stillness, my slightest thought
cancelled. This truth is so obvious that it is a wonder we
can forget it so often and so easily. The fact of it defines
who we are. To forget this is to forget who we are,
a species suffering from amnesia that bewildered seeks
its own name.

As long as we think that we can't achieve our potential, we will remain stuck in our comfort zone, never moving forward. In any case, it's simply not true: we all possess the potential to be a buddha. It's our nature.

Fight against greed, against aversion, against delusion—
they are the enemies. In the practice of Buddhism,
the path of the Buddha, we fight with the help of Dharma
and with patient endurance. We fight by resisting our
countless moods.

In one sense we journey alone, but in another we wake up together.

Suffering is not the feeling of fear, the desire for revenge, or the belief in the soul, it is *attachment* and *aversion* to those things—or any of a host of others.

There are two ways of looking at rituals. On the one hand, rituals are an external expression of our inner state. And on the other hand, we strengthen and reinforce our inner state by these external actions. Of course, in reality there are not two things, but rather a unified whole. As we practice together sincerely, we become increasingly aware that such notions as internal and external cannot be separated. This awareness is actually the growing realization of the real harmony that underlies everything.

True compassion is not just an emotional response but a firm commitment founded on reason.

Misfortune depresses us but at least makes us regard the world seriously; it provokes exploration and perhaps a reassessment of unwise habits. Pleasure and good fortune, on the other hand, immediately inspire us to throw down all defenses and to dote on a world we formerly mistrusted. Pain drives us—sometimes—to profound introspection and efforts of serious conviction; but pleasure—welcome pleasure floating sweetly through our senses—suggests a postponement of difficult matters: why *think*, now that happiness is here?

BHIKKHU NYANASOBHANO IN *LONGING FOR CERTAINTY*

Enlightenment is precisely the thorough abandonment of any notion of enlightenment; it is putting an end to the pursuit of happiness.

Past and future have their uses as tools of learning but our humanity does not need to be constantly oppressed by these linear concepts.

MU SOENG IN *TRUST IN MIND*

There are those who, hearing a word from a teacher, have a great enlightenment in which they lose their body and life. Some, alas, after three to five days resolve their doubts, while others take as much as three to five or even ten to twenty years before resolving their doubts. We tentatively give this period of doubt the name "grappling with one's koan." Though the words may differ and some may realize enlightenment quickly while others take a long time, when realization comes everyone wakes up to his original nature in its perfection. This realization is not based on words or phrases.

Mindfulness is the ultimate practice of nonaggression.

FRANK JUDE BOCCIO IN *MINDFULNESS YOGA*

Beings are owners of their actions, heirs of their actions, they originate from their actions, are bound to their actions, have their actions as their refuge. It is action that distinguishes beings as superior or inferior.

You can enter silence not by trying to enter but through the constant soft effort to let life be.

There can be right samadhi and wrong samadhi. Wrong samadhi is where the mind enters calm and there's no awareness at all. You can sit for two hours or even all day, but the mind doesn't know where it's been or what's happened. There is calm, but that's all. It's like a sharp knife that we don't bother to put to any use. This is a deluded type of calm, because there is not much awareness. Meditators may think they have reached the ultimate already, so they don't bother to look for anything else. Samadhi can be an enemy at this level. Wisdom cannot arise because there is no awareness of right and wrong. With right samadhi, no matter what level of calm is reached, there is awareness. There is full mindfulness and clear comprehension. This is the samadhi that gives rise to wisdom; one cannot get lost in it. Meditators should understand this.

Consequence is a fact of life; whatever we do, however slight, sets in motion a force we can never trace to its ultimate outcome. Regret comes to remind me of this truth.

True peace comes at a price, and the price is no self-pity and no self-delusion; the price is letting go of the small grasping self and putting in the time, effort, and perseverance to really see clearly; the price of true peace is patience and courage.

If the mere inflicting of physical pain were sufficient to make someone an enemy, you would have to consider your doctor an enemy, for he often causes pain during treatment. Now, as a genuine practitioner of compassion and bodhichitta, you must develop patience. And in order to practice sincerely and to develop patience, you need someone who willfully hurts you. People who willfully hurt us give us real opportunities to practice patience. They are testing our inner strength in a way that even our guru cannot. Even the Buddha possesses no such potential. Therefore, the enemy is *the only one* who gives us this golden opportunity. That is a remarkable conclusion, isn't it?

THE DALAI LAMA in *THE COMPASSIONATE LIFE*

As our meditations take us down into the dark unconscious of our minds, we disturb our own deepest fears and must face them ourselves. And we do not enter that underground world willingly. Our quest takes us there.

What would it be like if we could train ourselves to softly note "this is the deluded mind at work" each time an opinion is formed in the mind?

Chasing after fantasies is always a bad idea. Stick with reality. Reality's all you've got. But here's the real secret, the real miracle: It's enough.

Always adjust yourself to the others rather than expecting them to adjust to you. Then there is harmony.

To allow what is useful to come to hand we must patiently open our grasp and be willing to let go of methods that may no longer be effective.

Realizing emptiness eliminates the mistaken perception that there is no path to liberation.

Information collected on the subject of religion is worthless. Religion is, to the very end, something you must verify for yourself through actual practice.

We are all subject to praise and blame in almost every area of life—and we subject others to our own praise and blame as well. Praise and blame may seem to be opposites, but they in no way balance each other. Rather, both can function to separate us from other people. Praising others with an open heart is an affirming experience, but doing so with envy causes us spiritual contraction. When others' praise brings us confidence, it's nourishing, but when it evokes self-satisfaction, it distances us from others. Blame never has positive effects. Being the object of blame can elicit doubt and insecurity. But most destructive of all is blaming others, for it always separates *us* from *them*, even as it disempowers us by putting *them* in control of our emotions rather than taking responsibility for ourselves.

Whatever you consider beautiful, ugly, wonderful, tasty, or aromatic is simply a projection of your superstitious mind.

Without enthusiasm, we can't succeed at anything in our lives—especially buddhahood.

We cannot place the entire blame on politicians or those people who are seen as directly responsible for various situations; we too must bear some responsibility personally. It is only when the individual accepts personal responsibility that he or she begins to take some initiative. Just shouting and complaining is not good enough. A genuine change must first come from within the individual, then he or she can attempt to make significant contributions to humanity.

Truth can never be found in mere belief. Belief is restricted.
Truth is boundless.

Your conflicts with others are the result of fanatical, fixed ideas of good or bad.

If I do not struggle with the greed in my own heart, it is quite likely that, once in power, I too will be inclined to take advantage of the situation to serve my own interests. If I do not acknowledge the ill will in my own heart, I am more than likely to project it onto those who obstruct me. If I remain unaware that my sense of duality is a dangerous delusion, I will understand the problem of social change as the need for me to dominate the sociopolitical order. Add a conviction of my good intentions, along with a conviction of my superior understanding of the situation, and one has a recipe for disaster.

DAVID R. LOY in *THE GREAT AWAKENING*

Nonattachment means nonselfcentered responsiveness to a situation. Sometimes that will mean enduring unavoidable suffering and acknowledging that life is not under our control. But it also means taking appropriate action—talking to the neighbors, calling the landlord, and, if it comes to that, moving! All nonattachment precludes is increasing the suffering of others in order to minimize your own.

The Way is vast and wide. Don't restrict it.

Accepting, giving up, letting go—this is the way of lightness. Wherever you're clinging, there's becoming and birth right there.

We care passionately about the world, almost too much at times; this is understandable, as our very lives are at stake. But a deep and constantly refreshed nonattachment must lie at the core of any really passionate relationship. When this is forgotten, lost in the heat of caring, the relationship becomes deluded, self-centered, and blind—and ultimately unhelpful.

KEN JONES in THE NEW SOCIAL FACE OF BUDDHISM

Put on your armor of patience.

Supplication produces blessing, and although the blessing is often understood as something given to you, something that somehow engulfs you from outside, in fact blessing really isn't given to you at all. When you supplicate, you generate faith and devotion. That very faith and devotion cause the appearance of what we call blessing.

KHENCHEN THRANGU RINPOCHE in *CREATION AND COMPLETION*

In both Buddhist teachings and in the Yoga Upanishads, this tendency of the mind to jump around is referred to as "monkey mind"—and it can be very disconcerting to truly notice our own monkey mind for the first time. And yet, just seeing monkey mind as it is can be viewed as the first fruit of practice.

Reacting to anger is an addiction, pure and simple, just like smoking Marlboros. Objectively it takes more resources to keep smoking than to stop. Yet giving it up seems much harder than continuing, because you're addicted. But even the addiction of reacting to emotions isn't the root addiction. Ultimately, you are addicted to the idea of "you."

In the freshness and newness of each moment you can learn the heart's secret of falling in love over and over again.

Life has an endless supply of voices at its disposal when it wishes to call out to us. Do you have an equal number with which to respond?

Buddhist rebirth is not the same as reincarnation. It is axiomatic in Buddhism that there is no separate, eternal, or personal self to be reborn. Rebirth is a matter of cause and effect. The pathways of the intricate web of causation are never clear and apparent, and cannot be untangled in a linear manner so as to satisfy limited human rational faculties. But all actions do have results, and all these effects in turn have their impact, even if not apparent to us. In this sense rebirth occurs moment after moment. We take on the changing limitations of the life appearing before us as a result of having done so previously. We continue to identify ourselves in accord with the habits of our conditioned awareness and with the continuing production of illusions of this world that result from the intricate web of phenomenal causation. This happens moment after moment, day after day.

Karmic consciousness is endless, with nothing fundamental to rely on, including not others, not self, not sentient beings, and not causes or conditions. Although this is so, eating breakfast comes first.

If you try to remove lingering habits that come from attachment to form, not yet having seen into your own nature, you are like one in deep sleep trying to rid himself of a dream. The desire to rid oneself of a dream is itself a dream. The knowledge that it is a dream is also nothing but a dream. As for completely waking up from this sleep, no matter how much you seek something within a dream you will never attain it in reality.

All day long, we are living the life of the Buddha. Functioning in every way, we are in the midst of the operation of the Dharma. It is all us. We are all it. And this inseparable unity is the Sangha.

Before hurling insults and accusations at another, one should consider one's own state of mind and circumstances. The tendency to lash out, defame, and belittle is an aspect of conceit. The scriptures illustrate it with the image of a person enraged, taking up a handful of excrement to fling at his opponent. This person befouls himself even before the opponent. So, if there are matters on which we disagree, please let us all try to exercise patience and forgiveness in the spirit of the good-hearted.

Nonattachment does not mean indifference to the world or life—precisely the opposite. A profound experience of nonattachment is the ground on which we can build genuine compassion extending to all other sentient beings.

Practice allows us to discover that our happiness is not dependent on any of the things we once thought so crucial.

Questioning society's values is a great and important thing to do. But that's easy compared to questioning your own values. Questioning your own values means really questioning yourself, really looking at who and what you believe and who you are. Who are you?

To wake up is to realize that I am not *in* the world, I am what the world is doing right here and now.

Patience is not merely gritting our teeth and waiting for unwanted things to go away. Patience is a courageous state of mind that happily welcomes difficulty.

If there is any difficulty or problem, it's a problem of our own making.

Mutual respect is the foundation of genuine harmony.

Seeking it oneself with empty hands, you return with
    empty hands;
In that place where fundamentally nothing is acquired,
    you really acquire it.

It remains a wonder to me that if I really look at what is before me, I invariably give my heart to it.

Today's students of the Way go to teachers everywhere but they don't want to penetrate all the way to the bottom of the great matter. They journey to the east, west, north, and south, and take pride in having met many teachers. They try to surpass others with Zen stories and they collect paradoxical words and clever expressions from old masters. These are examples of the way of heretics.

What we mean by the sutras is the entire universe itself. There is no space nor time which is not the sutras. They use the words and letters of the ultimate truth as well as the words and letters of the worldly truth. They adopt the symbols of heavenly beings as well as those of human beings. They use the words and letters of beasts and asuras as well as those of hundreds of grasses and thousands of trees. For this reason, the long and short, the square and round, the blue and yellow, the red and white—marshalling solemnly in the ten directions of the universe—are undeniably the sutras' words and letters and faces. They are the instruments of the great Way and the scriptures for a Buddhist.

DECEMBER 2

To be unable to die is to be unable to live. By denying death we also deny life. Can we learn how to live by learning how to die?

Pain, like other sensations, can be our teacher. Approach pain with respect and an attitude of inquiry. Much of our suffering is a result of our avoidance of pain. Our practice is to observe our resistance to feeling pain, and learn ways to soften that resistance. Through this practice we learn that much of our pain is merely discomfort with the way things are. One thing we learn through practice is to more accurately sense what is real pain and what is discomfort.

FRANK JUDE BOCCIO IN *MINDFULNESS YOGA*

Compassion is the ability to see what needs doing right now and the willingness to do it right now. Sometimes compassion may even mean doing nothing at all.

Frustration, anger, hatred, and sadness are part of life. We cannot avoid them or dispel them. They are not the cause of suffering; our aversion to them is.

It isn't, for me, about being a Jew *or* a Buddhist, or a Jew *and* a Buddhist. It's about being a person paying attention to what works for me to keep my mind and heart peaceful, my life meaningful.

Let come whatever comes, let go all that goes.

This spiritual life, monks, does not have gain, honor, and renown for its benefit, or the attainment of moral discipline for its benefit, or the attainment of concentration for its benefit, or knowledge and vision for its benefit. But it is this unshakable liberation of mind that is the goal of this spiritual life, its heartwood, and its end.

Faith is one with the fruit of enlightenment; the fruit of enlightenment is one with faith.

Whether you notice your own enlightenment or not
is utterly inconsequential; whether you think you're
enlightened or not has nothing to do with the real state
of affairs.

Strong emotional reactions always signal the need to look more deeply at your beliefs.

EZRA BAYDA WITH JOSH BARTOK
IN *SAYING YES TO LIFE (EVEN THE HARD PARTS)*

Buddhist scriptures mention eighty-four thousand types of negative and destructive thoughts, which have eighty-four thousand corresponding approaches or antidotes. It is important not to have the unrealistic expectation that somehow, somewhere, we will find a single magic key that will help us eradicate all of these negativities.

In a deeper sense, not killing encourages vitality, energy, creative livelihood, and wonder. In accord with this precept we profoundly appreciate and are grateful for the awesome gift of just being alive. We violate the precept against killing whenever we discourage ourself or others from expressing the fullness of our being and love. When we see the world as estranged and alienated, merely a collection of dead objects to be manipulated or exploited to satisfy our selfish desires, we have killed the dynamic, vital world and its lively being, and have most fundamentally violated this precept.

The realization born of zazen is merely a fact, an experienced fact, in the same way that the taste of tea is a fact. A cup of tea has no thought, no idea, no philosophy. It tastes the same to Buddhists as it does to Christians.

Compassion and a good heart are not only important at the beginning but also in the middle and at the end.

If you want to believe in reincarnation, you have to believe that *this life,* what you're living through right now, *is* the afterlife. You're missing out on the afterlife you looked forward to in your last existence by worrying about your next life. *This* is what happens after you die. Take a look.

Above the heavens there is no Maitreya (the buddha of future birth), below the earth there is no Maitreya, but seeing his face is superior to hearing his name. If you meet him in person you cannot be deceived.

DECEMBER 18

Whenever we feel that we are definitely in the right, so much so that we refuse to open up to anything or anybody else, we've gone wrong. We're into wrong view. When suffering arises, where does it arise from? From wrong view.

No intoxicant clouds our minds more than the "never-enough" of consumerism.

DECEMBER 20

Complete liberation sounds like a big deal. And it is.
It's the biggest deal around. But don't make too much
of it—because it's also absolutely nothing at all.

DECEMBER 21

Even emptiness is empty.

DECEMBER 22

When my parents were alive and well, I grumbled
ceaselessly, and the words "I can't do it" were quick
to roll off my tongue. I came to notice, however, that
this "I can't do it" that I was forever mouthing was not,
in reality, an unbiased assessment of an objective
impossibility, but only a speculative impossibility based
upon my own assessment of my power at that moment.
When you feel you have a capacity of say, 10.0, anything
up to 9.9 feels possible; the feeling "I can't do it" arises just
at the point at which you are given a 10.1 assignment.
The person who is quick to judge a task as impossible will
never perform any task beyond a 10.0. That person will
never improve. For this reason, you must never think, "I
can't do it."

Compassion is the wish for another being to be free from suffering; love is wanting them to have happiness.

DECEMBER 24

The art of mutual giving also demands that we learn the art of receiving.

Jesus heard these words as he received baptism from John the Baptist at the river Jordan: "You are my Beloved, in whom I am well pleased." Sitting in stillness, a moment of grace may arrive wherein we are also able to hear these words resound throughout our whole being, and throughout the universe. Trembling, we ask, "Who, me?" And the answer is, "Yes, you!"

RUBEN L.F. HABITO in *LIVING ZEN, LOVING GOD*

DECEMBER 26

Each one of us, right where we sit, is continuously shining with the light of nonduality. Do you see it?

DECEMBER 27

Monks, what one intends and what one plans and whatever one has a tendency toward: this becomes a basis for the continuance of consciousness. Such is the origin of this whole mass of suffering. If, monks, one does not intend and does not plan but still has a tendency toward something, this becomes a basis for the continuance of consciousness. Such is the origin of this whole mass of suffering. But, monks, when one does not intend and does not plan and does not have a tendency toward anything, no basis exists for the continuance of consciousness. When there is no basis, there is no support for the establishing of consciousness. When consciousness is unestablished and does not come to growth, there is no production of future renewed existence. When there is no production of future renewed existence, future birth, aging-and-death, sorrow, lamentation, pain, dejection, and despair cease. Such is the cessation of this whole mass of suffering.

DECEMBER 28

Living from perceived boundaries creates imaginary prisons.

If we don't think rightly, if we don't practice rightly, we will fall back to being animals, creatures in hell, hungry ghosts, or demons. How is this? Just look in your mind. When anger arises, what is it? There it is, just look! When delusion arises, what is it? That's it, right there! When greed arises, what is it? Look at it right there! When the mind does not recognize and clearly understand these mental states, it ceases to be that of a human being. All conditions are in the state of "becoming." Becoming gives rise to "birth" or existence as determined by the present conditions. Thus we become and exist as our minds condition us.

Fasting does not mean refraining from the formal eating of food. It means refraining from feeding on the roots of delusion. Fasting means looking into your own nature and illuminating your consciousness, cutting off deluded feelings arising from analytical thinking, remaining apart from external phenomena and unattached to the internal void, completely purifying yourself so that things with no more than a thread of meaning become nonexistent in your life.

Whatever happens in your life and practice, just take note of it and keep going on that long and gentle walk. Remember who you are, and keep on going. And forget about that, and keep on going.

EPIGRAPH

What can I accomplish
Although not yet a Buddha?
Let my priest's body
be the raft to carry
sentient beings to the yonder shore.

EIHEI DOGEN (TRANS. STEVEN HEINE)

BIBLIOGRAPHY & INDEX BY BOOK CITED

All titles below published by Wisdom Publications.
NUMBERS IN BRACKETS INDICATE THE PAGES IN THIS VOLUME ON
WHICH EXCERPT FROM THIS TITLE APPEARS.

Among Tibetan Texts: History and Literature of the Himalayan Plateau. E. Gene Smith. Edited by Kurtis R. Schaeffer. 2001. [93]

The Art of Just Sitting: Essential Writings on the Zen Practice of Shikantaza. Second Edition. Edited by John Daido Loori. Introduced by Taigen Dan Leighton. 2004. [164, 248]

Awesome Nightfall: The Life, Times, and Poetry of Saigyo. William R. LaFleur. 2003. [27]

Bad Dog! A Memoir of Love, Beauty, and Redemption in Dark Places. Lin Jensen. 2005. [3, 38, 66, 101, 118, 182, 212, 236, 279, 294, 334]

Becoming the Compassion Buddha: Tantric Mahamudra for Everyday Life. Lama Thubten Yeshe. Edited by Robina Courtin. 2003. [6, 63, 83, 178, 211, 235, 280, 306, 309]

Becoming Vajrasattva: The Tantric Path of Purification. Lama Thubten Yeshe. Edited by Nicholas Ribush. 2004. [71, 94, 140, 167, 185, 202, 240, 305]

Beside Still Waters: Jews, Christians, and the Way of the Buddha. Edited by Harold Kasimow, John P. Keenan, and Linda Klepinger Keenan. 2003. [341]

Blue Jean Buddha: Voices of Young Buddhists. Edited by Sumi Loundon. 2001. [8, 69]

The Book of Equanimity: Illuminating Classic Zen Koans. Gerry Shishin Wick. 2005. [114, 141, 204, 219, 250, 278, 295, 312, 361]

Creation and Completion: Essential Points of Tantric Meditation. Jamgon Kongtrul Lodro Thaye. Introduced, translated, and annotated by Sarah Harding. Commentary by Khenchen Thrangu Rinpoche. 2002. [39, 112, 120, 155, 203, 214, 238, 262, 316]

The Compassionate Life. Tenzin Gyatso, the Fourteenth Dalai Lama. 2003. [1, 65, 138, 180, 241, 275, 285, 296, 307, 326, 332, 347, 350, 358]

Daughters of Emptiness: Poems of Chinese Buddhist Nuns. Beata Grant. 2003. [60]

The Dharma of Dragons and Daemons: Buddhist Themes in Modern Fantasy. David R. Loy and Linda Goodhew. 2004. [14, 117, 194, 264, 297, 337]

The Dharma of Star Wars. Matthew Bortolin. 2005. [20, 104, 137, 181, 184, 229, 257, 283, 340]

Dogen's Extensive Record: A Translation of the Eihei Koroku. Translated by Taigen Dan Leighton and Shohaku Okumura. Edited and introduced by Taigen Dan Leighton. Introductory essays by Steven Heine and John Daido Loori. 2004. [37, 52, 125, 165, 266, 322, 352]

Eihei Dogen: Mystical Realist. Hee-Jin Kim. 2004. [11, 97, 158, 188, 205, 216, 244, 263, 336, 344]

Essence of the Heart Sutra: The Dalai Lama's Heart of Wisdom Teachings. Tenzin Gyatso, the Fourteenth Dalai Lama. Translated and edited by Geshe Thupten Jinpa. 2002. [47, 59, 87, 175, 200, 218, 233, 255, 273]

Essentials of Mahamudra: Looking Directly at the Mind. Khenchen Thrangu Rinpoche. 2004. [99, 170]

Everything Yearned For: Manhae's Poems of Love and Longing. Translated and introduced by Francisca Cho. 2005. [45, 209]

Faces of Compassion: Classic Bodhisattva Archetypes and Their Modern Expression. Taigen Dan Leighton. 2003. [25, 86, 172, 186, 272, 301, 321, 348, 356, 359]

Food for the Heart: The Collected Teachings of Ajahn Chah. Introduced by Ajahn Amaro. 2002. [17, 23, 56, 128, 135, 150, 174, 197, 225, 253, 269, 281, 293, 313, 353, 364]

The Four Noble Truths (Volume 1 of the Foundation of Buddhist Thought). Geshe Tashi Tsering. Edited by Gordon McDougall. 2005. [12, 109]

The Gateless Gate: The Classic Book of Zen Koans. Translated with commentary by Koun Yamada. 2004. [48, 162, 271]

The Great Awakening: A Buddhist Social Theory. David R. Loy. 2003. [40, 122, 161, 206, 220, 246, 310, 329, 354]

Great Disciples of the Buddha: Their Lives, Their Works, Their Legacy. Nyanaponika Thera and Hellmuth Hecker. Edited and introduced by Bhikkhu Bodhi. 2003. [31, 90]

Hardcore Zen: Punk Rock, Monster Movies, and the Truth About Reality. Brad Warner. 2003. [7, 30, 67, 183, 213, 239, 258, 261, 277, 299, 308, 318, 328, 339, 345, 351, 355]

How to Raise an Ox: Zen Practice as Taught in Master Dogen's Shobogenzo. Francis Dojun Cook. 2002. [64, 136, 198, 226, 254]

In the Buddha's Words: An Anthology of Discourses from the Pali Canon. Edited by Bhikkhu Bodhi. 2005. [58, 84, 106, 132, 195, 232, 259, 291, 343, 362]

In This Very Life: The Liberation Teachings of the Buddha. Sayadaw U Pandita. Translated by Venerable U Aggacitta. Edited by Kate Wheeler. 1991. [9, 95, 159, 325]

Journey to Mindfulness: The Autobiography of Bhante G. Bhante Henepola Gunaratana with Jeanne Malmgren. 2003. [54, 75, 127, 147]

Like A Dream, Like A Fantasy: The Zen Teaching and Poetry of Nyogen Senzaki. Nyogen Senzaki. Edited and introduced by Eido Shimano. 2005. [43, 126, 149, 208, 249]

Living Zen, Loving God. Ruben L.F. Habito. 2004. [80, 123, 143, 196, 360]

Longing for Certainty: Reflections on the Buddhist Life. Bhikkhu Nyanasobhano. 2003. [32, 68, 110, 286]

Medicine & Compassion: A Tibetan Lama's Guidance for Caregivers. Chokyi Nyima Rinpoche with David R. Shlim, M.D. Translated by Erik Pema Kunsang. 2004. [2, 79, 130, 152, 315]

Mindfulness Yoga: The Awakened Union of Breath, Body, and Mind. Frank Jude Boccio. 2004. [21, 81, 131, 199, 290, 317, 338]

Mind Training: The Great Collection. Translated and edited by Thupten Jinpa. 2005. Compiled by Shünu Gyalchuk and Könchok Gyaltsen. [16, 82, 171, 231]

Mud and Water: The Collected Teachings of Zen Master Bassui. Translated by Arthur Braverman. 2002. [15, 76, 146, 173, 193, 224, 245, 268, 289, 323, 335, 365]

The New Social Face of Buddhism: A Call to Action. Ken Jones. 2003. [107, 115, 142, 314]

Nixon Under the Bodhi Tree and Other Works of Buddhist Fiction. Edited by Kate Wheeler. 2004. [41, 55, 92, 189]

Novice to Master: An Ongoing Lesson in the Extent of My Own Stupidity. Soko Morinaga. Translated from the Japanese by Belenda Attaway Yamakawa. 2004. [5, 26, 61, 179, 210, 234, 274, 303, 357]

Now! The Art of Being Truly Present. Jean Smith. 2004. [4, 62, 108, 177, 252, 304]

The Nyingma School of Tibetan Buddhism: Its Fundamentals and History. Dudjom Rinpoche. Translated and edited by Gyurme Dorje and Matthew Kapstein. 1991. [33]

On Zen Practice: Body, Breath, and Mind. Edited by Taizan Maezumi and Bernie Glassman. Revised by Wendy Egyoku Nakao and John Daishin Buksbazen. 2002. [24, 85, 270, 284, 300, 324, 331, 349]

Opening the Hand of Thought: Foundations of Zen Buddhist Practice. Kosho Uchiyama. Translated and edited by Daitsu Tom Wright, Jisho Warner, and Shohaku Okumura. 2004. [42, 98, 121, 160, 190]

Ordinary Mind: Exploring the Common Ground of Zen and Psychoanalysis. Barry Magid. 2005. [34, 89, 119, 156, 201, 221, 237, 276, 287, 311, 320, 327]

Practicing the Path: A Commentary on the Lamrim Chenmo. Yangsi Rinpoche. Translated by Tsering Tuladhar. Edited by Miranda Adams. 2003. [74, 134, 157, 302]

Practicing Wisdom: The Perfection of Shantideva's Bodhisattva Way. Tenzin Gyatso, the Fourteenth Dalai Lama. Translated and edited by Geshe Thupten Jinpa. 2005. [50, 124, 153, 207, 247]

Psychoanalysis and Buddhism: An Unfolding Dialogue. Edited by Jeremy D. Safran. 2003. [53, 96, 73, 133, 176, 215, 242]

Pure and Simple: The Extraordinary Teachings of a Thai Buddhist Laywoman. Upasika Kee Nanayon. Translated and introduced by Thanissaro Bhikkhu. 2005. [51, 145, 191]

Reason's Traces: Identity and Interpretation in Indian and Tibetan Buddhist Thought. Matthew T. Kapstein. 2001. [35, 70, 111]

The Record of Transmitting the Light: Zen Master Keizan's Denkoroku. Translated by Francis Dojun Cook. 2003. [166, 187, 243, 333]

Saying Yes to Life (Even the Hard Parts). Ezra Bayda (with Josh Bartok). 2005. [46, 78, 103, 113, 148, 168, 223, 251, 267, 292, 346, 363]

Shingon Refractions: Myoe and the Mantra of Light. Mark Unno. 2004. [72]

Spiritual Friends: Meditations by Monks and Nuns of the International Mahayana Institute. Edited by Thubten Dondrub. 2001. [28, 88]

The State of Mind Called Beautiful. Sawadaw U Pandita. Edited and introduced by Kate Wheeler. 2006. [154, 342]

Steps on the Path to Enlightenment: A Commentary on Tsongkhapa's Lamrim Chenmo. Volume 1: The Foundation Practices. Geshe Lhundub Sopa. Edited by David Patt and Beth Newman. 2004. [116, 144]

Steps on the Path to Enlightenment: A Commentary on Tsongkhapa's Lamrim Chenmo. Volume 2: Karma. Geshe Lhundub Sopa with David Patt. 2005. [49, 163]

The Three Levels of Spiritual Perception: An Oral Commentary on The Three Visions (Snang gsum) of Ngorchen Konchog Lhundrub. Deshung Rinpoche. Translated by Jared Rhoton. Edited and introduced by Victoria R. M. Scott. 2003. [10, 44]

Trust in Mind: The Rebellion of Chinese Zen. Mu Soeng. 2004. [102, 192, 222, 260, 288, 298]

Uniting Wisdom and Compassion: Illuminating the Thirty-Seven Practices of a Bodhisattva. Chokyi Dragpa. Introduced by Chokyu Nyima Rinpoche. Translated by Heidi I. Koppl. 2004. [19, 57, 228]

Waking Up Together: Intimate Partnership on the Spiritual Path. Ellen and Charles Birx. 2005. [18, 77, 129, 169, 227, 256, 282, 319]

The Way of Awakening: A Commentary on Shantideva's Bodhicharyavatara. Geshe Yeshe Tobden. Edited by Fiorella Rizzi. Translated from the Italian by Manu Bazzano and Sarita Doveton. 2005. [151]

Where the World Does Not Follow: Buddhist China in Picture and Poem. Translated and introduced by Mike O'Connor. 2002. [36, 265]

Who Ordered This Truckload of Dung? Inspiring Stories for Welcoming Life's Difficulties. Ajahn Brahm. 2005. [29, 91, 139]

The Wisdom of Listening. Edited by Mark Brady. 2003. [13, 100, 217]

Zen Meditation in Plain English. John Daishin Buksbazen. 2002. [22, 105, 230, 366]

INDEX BY TOPIC

absolute and relative 39, 47, 60, 70,
    162, 207, 336
acceptance 2, 6, 137, 148, 169, 204,
    209, 215, 237, 313
addiction 318
anger 44, 52, 84, 124, 151, 203, 252,
    275, 318, 325, 340
appearance and reality 126, 207
attachment 11, 57, 58, 124, 181,
    184, 200, 211, 246, 251, 283
attitude 1, 6, 12, 32, 40, 63, 69, 74,
    83, 87, 106, 130, 142, 151, 152,
    185, 200, 237, 251, 270
authority 103
Avalokiteshvara 83
aversion 174, 200, 222, 261, 283,
    338, 340

being-time 264, 329
belief 168
beginner's mind 8
blame 134, 304
blindmen and the elephant (parable)
    232
bodhisattva activity 19, 34, 57, 61,
    86, 100, 107, 192

bondage 56, 85
bowing 42
breakfast 322
breath 123, 159
Buddha 13, 31, 92, 163, 167, 169,
    268, 296, 352
buddha nature 24, 173, 280

change 62, 88, 154, 236
charioteer 54
choice 184, 269
Christ 80
Christians 349
cobra 17
cold 37
compassion 50, 59, 65, 79, 87, 100, 119,
    129, 142, 153, 163, 192, 201, 212,
    260, 267, 285, 326, 339, 350, 358
conceiving 259
conflict 255, 309
confusion 23, 253
continuous practice 64
courage 104, 210, 295, 330

daily life 34, 63, 96, 105
dark side 104

death 32, 36, 68, 147, 209, 217, 254, 337
dedication of merit 157
delusion 48, 119, 140, 145, 146, 160, 168, 170, 207, 243, 295, 298, 310, 328
desire 50, 122, 160
determination 234
Dharma 97, 127, 163, 226, 253, 269
Dharma transmission 183
Diamond Sutra 208
diligence 164
discomfort 338
doubt 67, 128
dreams 170, 228, 323

earth 279
eating 52
effort 214, 256, 274, 280, 357
ego 62, 168
elephant and the blindman (parable) 232
emptiness 34, 36, 47, 50, 60, 73, 165, 214, 242, 265, 302, 356
enemies 16, 171, 241, 281, 296
enlightenment 7, 15, 27, 33, 48, 59, 61, 64, 76, 96, 97, 113, 121, 132, 143, 149, 156, 163, 169, 190, 196, 213, 218, 243, 268, 274, 287, 342, 345, 352, 355

enthusiasm 306
equanimity 17, 79, 132, 193, 204
"everyday is a good day" (koan) 80
evil 229, 255
expectations 222

faith 46, 102, 198, 315, 344
falling 38
fantasies 140, 299, 323
fasting 365
fear 29, 91, 180, 251, 283, 351, 297
fiction 41, 189
forgiveness 177
form and emptiness 47, 60, 126, 221, 323
freedom (see also liberation) 56, 82, 85
future lives 172, 351

generosity 359
giving and receiving 359
goals 7, 146
God 123
good heart 100, 350
grace 360
grasping 50
gratitude 4, 334
greed 310, 354

happiness 1, 9, 12, 20, 28, 286, 327
harmony 284, 300, 332, 356
hatred 84
hell 6, 36, 44, 107, 140
history 90

ignorance 4, 208, 255, 256, 260, 273, 275, 310
ill will 310
impermanence 62, 68, 88, 133, 147, 181, 236,
imaginary numbers 53
Indra's Net 186
insults 325
intellectual understanding 94, 143, 150
intention 40, 116, 205
interdependence 35, 115, 154, 161, 236, 239, 279
interpenetration 37, 80, 154, 208, 236, 244, 272, 279, 329
intoxicants 354
itinerancy 30, 135, 335

Jesus 80, 360
joy 9, 11
Judaism 341
justice 40

karma 10, 28, 49, 66, 81, 130 134, 151, 171, 178, 216, 220, 235, 244, 250, 252, 256, 264, 272, 277, 291, 294, 307, 321, 322
knowing 72
koans 15, 77, 80
koan study 289

letting go 21, 92
liberation 58, 82, 101, 108, 137, 194, 247, 251, 269, 274, 302, 312, 343, 355, 363
listening 77, 100
life 3, 219, 254, 336
logic 93, 230
love 18, 20, 21, 45, 62, 65, 77, 129, 164, 177, 181, 209, 251, 319, 334, 358
loving-kindness 2, 79
luck 286, 287

Maitreya 352
materialism 52, 92, 122, 206, 354
meat-eating 81
medicine 71, 73
meditation 11, 34, 41, 50, 71, 98, 105, 121, 128, 149, 160, 193, 213, 215, 221, 227, 249, 265, 316, 297, 342

mind 9, 17, 19, 26, 36, 76, 84, 89, 93, 106, 112, 120, 131, 138, 145, 154, 155, 159, 170, 187, 189, 218, 238, 243, 245, 247, 262, 267, 298, 331, 364
mind and body 247
mindfulness 19, 36, 95, 99, 158, 225, 262, 290
mind training 16, 191, 298
monkey mind 316

nirvana 31, 70, 117, 137, 138, 159, 240, 246, 313
nonattachment 15, 56, 57, 58, 64, 133, 176, 184, 206, 248, 261, 270, 274, 311, 314, 326, 342
nonchoosing 174, 200, 261, 340
nonduality 29, 70, 80, 96, 240, 247, 276, 278, 284, 334, 361
nonexpression 263
nonharming 16, 81, 84, 106, 144, 224, 229, 290, 348
noninterfering 17, 225
nonjudging 112, 145, 166, 197, 223, 338, 305, 312, 342
nonstriving 89, 146, 149, 194, 248
no-self 5, 35, 36, 53, 60, 111, 168, 189, 201, 261, 265, 318, 333

nonthinking 17, 99, 114, 140, 155, 193, 259, 278
not-knowing 72, 120, 141, 187
now 158, 166, 269, 277, 286, 329

old age 98
omniscience 72
oneness 37, 324

pain 44, 91, 261, 296, 336
paradox 48, 192
path 3, 14, 91, 282, 312, 366
patience 38, 295, 301, 315, 325, 330
peace 23, 104, 295
play 194
poems 27, 36, 42, 45, 209, 265
politics 307, 308, 309, 314, 320, 325
practice 64, 78, 125, 135, 136, 145, 146, 150, 156, 160, 189, 199, 295, 303, 327, 366
praise 304
prayer 78
precepts 81, 224, 348, 354
problems 22, 26, 30, 105, 141, 182, 241, 276, 330, 331
punishment 40

questioning 8, 67, 326

rainbows 57, 126
rebirth 195, 313, 321, 351, 362, 364
refuge 25, 102, 127, 163, 167, 291
regret 294
reincarnation 172, 259, 321, 351, 364
relationships 227, 256, 282
religion 175, 303
renunciation 54, 202
respect 332
responsibility 59, 61, 79, 82, 134, 171, 229, 235, 256, 271, 291, 307, 331
right action 4, 68, 75, 81, 109, 119, 142, 144, 161, 271, 320, 339
right effort 4, 135, 164, 257, 306, 357
right speech 13, 110, 125, 233, 263, 304, 325, 353
right view 352
righteousness 252
ritual 25, 42, 284, 315
robes 75
rocks and trees, teachings of 226

samadhi 179, 188, 266, 293
samsara 31, 70, 117, 138, 241, 246
Sangha 52, 163, 300, 324, 336, 347
scripture 336, 347
sectarianism 173, 232

self and other 43, 52, 65, 83, 109, 167, 180, 201, 223, 239, 243, 250, 256, 275, 278, 279, 334, 359, 363
selfing (verb) 66
sensualism 9
sickness 68, 108, 139
silence 55, 118, 249, 263, 292
skillful means 233, 301, 347
sleep 130
"sound of one hand clapping" (koan) 77
squashes 98
suffering 7, 20, 21, 22, 28, 51, 74, 80, 106, 180, 211, 229, 261, 267, 273, 283, 286, 296, 362
supernatural powers 72, 76, 245
superstition 305
supplication 315
stupidity 26

teachers 14, 46, 84, 103, 125, 126, 226, 233, 270, 335
thoughts 155, 262
three refuges 25, 163
three treasures 324
thusness 7, 27, 30, 33, 43, 89, 97, 102, 104, 113, 115, 131, 165, 169, 197, 204, 213, 215, 219, 237, 242, 292, 299, 333, 342, 349, 361
time 90, 158, 166, 172, 258, 264, 277, 288, 329

tooth-cleaner 205
training 298
transformation 63, 83, 122, 136, 147, 154, 157, 185, 198, 218, 236
true self 89, 114, 126, 148, 215, 242, 243
trust 3, 102
truth 39, 226, 308, 336

unconscious 130, 297
undeclared statements 132

vegetarianism 81
vocation 199

war 255
washing 63
water 60, 268
wisdom 76, 128, 145, 196, 203, 206, 223, 260
wrong samadhi 293
wrong view 353

yoga 21, 199

zazen (see also meditation) 11, 36, 38, ,98, 105, 121, 123, 149, 160, 188, 193, 213, 221, 266, 349

**Saying Yes to Life
(Even the Hard Parts)**
Ezra Bayda with Josh Bartok
Foreword by Thomas Moore
272 pages, ISBN 0-86171-274-9,
$15.00

"Ezra Bayda is one of our favorite
Buddhist teachers. In his first two
books, he demonstrated a keen
ability to make spiritual practice
out of any and all experiences. In
this astonishing collection of
sayings and short meditations,
Bayda delivers profound Buddhist
wisdom laced with simplicity,
practicality, depth, and inspira-
tional vitality."—*Spirituality and
Health*

Daily Wisdom
365 Buddhist Inspirations
Edited by Josh Bartok
384 pages,
ISBN 0-86171-300-1, $16.95

Daily Wisdom draws on the richness of Buddhist writings to offer a spiritual cornucopia that will illuminate and inspire day after day, year after year. Sources span a spectrum from ancient sages to modern teachers, from monks to lay people, from East to West, from poetry to prose. Each page, and each new day, reveals another gem of *Daily Wisdom.*

NOW!
The Art of Being
Truly Present
Jean Smith
144 pages, ISBN 0-86171-480-6,
$14.00

NOW! offers 85 original reflections, each paired with "mindful reminders," on subjects we all deal with on a daily basis and throughout our lives: Work, Aging, Gossip, Sex, Friendship, and more.

"A spiritual companion we can all use to find ideas for enriching our daily lives and recognizing happiness. Thank you Jean Smith for these reminders on how to be here NOW."—Barbara Ann Kipfer, author of *14,000 things to be happy about*

ABOUT WISDOM

Wisdom Publications, a nonprofit publisher, is dedicated to making available authentic Buddhist works for the benefit of all. We publish translations of the sutras and tantras, commentaries and teachings of past and contemporary Buddhist masters, and original works by the world's leading Buddhist scholars. We publish our titles with the appreciation of Buddhism as a living philosophy and with the special commitment to preserve and transmit important works from all the major Buddhist traditions.

To learn more about Wisdom, or to browse books online, visit our website at wisdompubs.org. You may request a copy of our mail-order catalog online or by writing to this address:

Wisdom Publications
199 Elm Street
Somerville, Massachusetts 02144 USA
Telephone: (617) 776-7416
Fax: (617) 776-7841
Email: info@wisdompubs.org
www.wisdompubs.org

THE WISDOM TRUST

As a nonprofit publisher, Wisdom is dedicated to the publication of fine Dharma books for the benefit of all sentient beings and dependent upon the kindness and generosity of sponsors in order to do so. If you would like to make a donation to Wisdom, please do so through our Somerville office. If you would like to sponsor the publication of a book, please write or email us at the address above.

Thank you.

Wisdom is a nonprofit, charitable 501(c)(3) organization affiliated with the Foundation for the Preservation of the Mahayana Tradition (FPMT).